MICHAEL BRAUN

CAN I TRUST GOD?

UNDERSTANDING THE BOOK OF JOB

Unless otherwise indicated, all Scripture quotations are taken from The New King James Version. Copyright © 1979, 1981, 1982 by Thomas Nelson, Inc. Used by permission. All rights reserved.

Scripture quotations marked TPT are taken from Letters from Heaven by the Apostle Paul, The Passion Translation TM, copyright © 2013. Used by permission of 5 Fold Media, LLC, Syracuse, NY 13039, United States of America. All rights reserved.

Scripture quotations marked KJV are taken from The King James Version of the Bible.

All emphasis within Scripture quotations is the author's own.

Can I Trust God?

ISBN: 978-0-692-34664-8

Copyright © 2015

Published by Michael Braun

Prepared for publishing by:

Orion Productions, LLC.
PO Box 51194
Colorado Springs, CO 80949
www.orion316.tv

Editor: Cande Maxie

Printed in the United States of America. This book or parts thereof may not be reproduced in any form, stored in a retrieval system, or transmitted in any form by any means—electronic, mechanical, photocopy, recording, or otherwise—without prior written permission from the Publisher.

DEDICATION

I would like to dedicate this book to everyone who has attempted to defend the character of God only to hear the response, "Well, what about Job?"

Like me, you probably did not have an immediate answer to that question. Consider this book to be a thoughtful response. Be encouraged, you were not wrong: God is only good. Anyone who has believed differently has been deceived! I bless you for knowing the truth and not backing down. We are truly one in Spirit!

Your brother in the knowledge of the goodness of God,

Michael Braun

ACKNOWLEDGEMENTS

I would like to thank most of all my friend and editor, Cande Maxie. No one but she will know the countless hours needed to make this book both simple and, hopefully, liberating. If you are able to receive revelation from these pages it is due in large part to her perseverance through countless challenges.

I would like to thank Ms. Louise Leigh for her indispensable edits and constructive insights.

I would also like to thank the following proof readers who all contributed to changes in the final edition: Tom and Mary Beth Peoples, Christy Schadoff, Maxine Grace, and Caleb Braun.

TABLE OF CONTENTS

	A Word from the Author	9
	Foreword	11
	Introduction	13
Chapter 1	Why is This Love Letter Under Attack?	17
Chapter 2	Why is the Meaning of "Sovereignty" a Target?	29
Chapter 3	Why Do We Long to Trust God?	43
Chapter 4	Is it God's Fault?	59
Chapter 5	How Does God Deal With Our Deceived Hearts?	75
Chapter 6	What is Job's Mindset?	93
Chapter 7	How Can We Understand Theology Through Relationship?	109
Chapter 8	What is True Rest?	123
Chapter 9	Vital Life Lessons from Job	139
Chapter 10	Job's Confessions of Confusion	155
Chapter 11	Explaining Controversial Passages in Job — Part 1	171
Chapter 12	Job Meets God	183

Chapter 13	Explaining Controversial Passages in Job — Part 2	195
Chapter 14	Summarizing the Powerful Lessons from Job	203
	Prayer	215
	About the Author	221

A WORD FROM THE AUTHOR

The purpose of this book is to reveal the goodness of God. Primarily, I will do this by exposing how the book of Job has been used to malign God's character. As you receive revelation of God's goodness you may condemn yourself over some past experience because you did not know this sooner. This strategy of the enemy will only be effective if you allow yourself to agree with his condemnation. **If your thoughts are self-condemning then they cannot be from God!** *"Therefore submit to God. <u>Resist the devil</u> and he will flee from you"* (James 4:7). Hind sight is perfect, and we all have done, and will do, things without complete understanding. Don't be sidetracked into condemning yourself and miss the revelation of God's goodness. God does not hold our ignorance against us. As we continue to pursue a relationship with Him, He is patient with all of us who, without exception, are learning as we go.

Our heavenly Father is good and His thoughts toward us are nothing but good. *"For I know the thoughts that I think toward you, says the LORD, thoughts of peace and not of evil, to give you a future and a hope"* (Jeremiah 29:11). If you begin to think that some circumstance was all your fault or you could have prevented something from happening, then forgive yourself quickly and do not dwell upon it. This book is meant to bring you freedom as you discover the goodness of your God, not shame or condemnation. *"Now the Lord is the Spirit, and where the Spirit of the Lord is, there is freedom"* (2 Corinthians 3:17 RSV).

We can easily find scriptural proof that God does not blame us nor does He condemn us.

"And you, who once were alienated and enemies in your mind by wicked works, yet now He has reconciled in the body of His flesh through death, to present you holy, and <u>blameless</u>, and <u>above reproach</u> in His sight —" (Colossians 1:21-22).

"Just as He chose us in Him before the foundation of the world, that we should be holy and <u>without blame</u> before Him in love" (Ephesians 1:4).

"There is therefore now <u>no condemnation</u> to those who are in Christ Jesus, who do not walk according to the flesh, but according to the Spirit. For the law of the Spirit of life in Christ Jesus has made me free from the law of sin and death" (Romans 8:1-2).

"For God did <u>not send</u> His Son into the world <u>to condemn</u> the world, but that the world through Him might be saved" (John 3:17).

FOREWORD

I am honored to recommend this ground breaking work that Mike Braun has authored called "Can I Trust God?" This book is not only relevant for our generation, but, is vital to understand if we are going to see hearts transformed with the true message of the gospel. Who you think God is, is who you will proclaim Him to be!

This book will help you develop an accurate assessment of who God is, and that He is always worthy of your trust! The revelation of the goodness of God will keep you from trusting in yourself. Discover through this ancient story of Job how much God loves you, instead of loving what you do "for Him."

This well written book will cheerfully go into my library to be re-read and to be used as a reference resource.

Thank you Mike for your willingness to trust the Lord through your own journey! It is awesome to see how He has brought you to this place of abounding grace, and unending trust. He is worthy of all praise!

Daniel Amstutz

Director of Charis Bible College's School of Worship and School of Healing

INTRODUCTION

The story of Job is the Biblical account of a brief, turbulent period in one man's life. You may or may not have heard of Job, but somehow he has become one of the most controversial people of all time. Often when I mention writing about Job, people get a very apprehensive look on their face and make comments like: "Ooh, Job." Ironically, this is about the same reaction I would receive if I had told someone I had found a snake in their yard. I believe this bizarre foreboding is due to the many deceptions which surround Job's story. God's word should produce freedom. If God's word ever feels oppressive, then be assured an enemy is at work. I believe the apprehension surrounding Job is in response to how often the book has been used to deceive people about the character of God.

We were created to live in a trusting relationship with God who is our heavenly Father and without this relationship we will always feel insecure. Using the story of Job I will expose the deceptions Satan uses to undermine our trust in God. Job is the perfect book to teach us about trust because Job seems to be obsessed with rest and I am going to use his story to explain that our desire for rest and our desire for trust are one and the same. An inner longing of the human heart is to feel safe. This inner need for security can only be met by trusting God. **Job's story exposes what happens to somebody who believes he cannot trust God.** Without trusting God, Job can never find the rest he is searching for. To one degree or another this is the same restless condition in which most of us live our lives. Job's story can help us find genuine rest by answering the most important question of all: <u>**Can I trust God**</u>?

We will never fully trust God until His character is firmly established in our hearts. Satan is aware that the knowledge of what God is really like is the first step in the process of liberating our hearts. Therefore, he focuses on undermining the character of God, which is precisely the reason the book of Job is so controversial. Job believes he knows God, yet he is unaware that he has been deceived about God's character. **On some level, all of us have been deceived about God's character.** Like Job, these deceptions can subvert our relationship with God to the extent that we feel He is not trustworthy. As believers, we are ashamed to admit we don't trust God as much as we know we could.

One extremely vital contribution of Job's story is that it exposes trust as a fundamental human need that <u>must</u> be satisfied. Because Job had been deceived into believing God was not trustworthy, he attempted to fulfill that need through other means. Job's substitute for trusting God was to trust in himself to provide the security he so desperately needed. Because many of us chose this same option, the lessons in Job are extraordinarily applicable to us today.

> "For the thing I greatly feared has come upon me,
> And what I dreaded has happened to me.
> I am not at ease, nor am I quiet;
> I have no <u>rest</u>, for trouble comes." Job 3:25-26.

God is good and only good.
<u>Anything</u>
you have ever heard differently about Him is a lie!

CHAPTER 1

WHY IS THIS LOVE LETTER UNDER ATTACK?

Why is God's character the key?

<u>I believe an accurate understanding of God's character is the key to understanding the book of Job.</u> Misunderstanding God's character will cause us to draw wrong conclusions which can prove toxic to our spiritual growth. I John 4:16 makes a bold statement, *"God is love."* Because God is love, He is unable to act outside of His own character, which is love. 1 Corinthians 13:4-8a gives us the attributes of love which are also the attributes of God Himself. *"Love suffers long and is kind; love does not envy; love does not parade itself, is not puffed up; does not behave rudely, does not seek its own, is not provoked, thinks no evil; does not rejoice in iniquity, but rejoices in the truth; bears all things, believes all things, hopes all things, endures all things. Love never fails."* Every one of these attributes of love is an attribute of God Who is love.

The book of Job must be a love letter, because it was written by Love for the objects of His affection (us) to be read later. By approaching Job from this position we thereby lay a framework for practical answers and implementation in our lives. To approach the book of Job from any position other than an absolute assurance of God's love is to invite deception. According to God's own word, our faith must rest in the foundation of the goodness of God, or it does not qualify for faith at all. This is stated in Hebrews 11:6, *"But without faith it is impossible to please Him,* *for he who comes to God must believe that He is, and that <u>He is a rewarder</u> of those who diligently seek Him."*

God can only act like Himself. Any other conclusion is only the result of misunderstanding <u>the truth</u> of what He is really like.

To achieve answers that are grounded in truth requires that we adhere to a belief system which will not allow us to perceive God acting outside of His character of love. We must not allow our perception of God's actions to deviate from the unchangeable standard of God's own character. To do otherwise is an attempt to measure God using a moving scale based on opinion without scriptural foundation. James 1:17 says, *"Every good and perfect gift is from above, and comes down from the Father of lights, <u>with whom there is no variation or shadow of turning</u>."*

In short, since God cannot change, we only need to find the standard of His character and determine all of our answers from that one standard which is love. This standard was fully displayed when Jesus gave His life sacrificially for mankind. *"Greater love has no one than this, than to lay down one's life for his friends"* (John 15:13). God can only act like Himself. Any other conclusion is only the result of misunderstanding <u>the truth</u> of what He is really like.

Is the book of Job relevant today?

It is estimated by most Bible scholars that Job lived after the time of Noah, but before the time of Abraham. This means Job lived roughly 4000 years ago, making his story one of the oldest recorded in history. This brings up the question, "Is a study of the book of Job relevant for us today?" In any group of Christians I have surveyed, 90% have had a discussion with someone that mentioned the story of Job. Any subject that is commonly discussed after 4,000 years has clearly stood the test of time. The problem with teaching Job is not the relevance of the discussions it generates, but the fact that the emotions behind the discussions can become so passionate. The topics the book brings to the forefront are literally so relevant and so emotionally charged that almost everyone ardently defends his position. Most positions held on Job center around our perceptions of our heavenly Father.

What our heavenly Father is like and how we relate to Him is the single most important subject of our lives.

Two Christians arguing about Job is the equivalent of two siblings arguing about the character of their daddy. The proof of how desperately we desire to trust our heavenly Father is revealed by how quickly we rush to His defense. What our heavenly Father is like and how we relate to Him is the single most important subject of our lives. This makes the book of Job one of the most important stories ever recorded. An argument over the book of Job has to be understood from the foundation of the argument itself. The conflicts over Job are about one core question of the human heart: "Can I trust God?"

What makes Job the most unique book of the Bible?

Job is the longest book in the Bible devoted to events in one person's life. Although the books of Isaiah and Jeremiah are longer, they do not deal exclusively with the events of the authors' lives. Those books focus on the history of the Hebrew nation. The book of Job's extended focus on one individual is unprecedented in the word of God. Since God is intentional in

His actions, why would He give so much attention to the events in one person's life? What is the purpose of this love letter that God has left for us to read? Furthermore, since God is omniscient the fact that this book would be confusing to future readers did not escape Him. There must be something of great importance to be learned from Job or God would not have taken the known risk of the book's manipulation by His enemy.

Job is also unique in that it contains more dialogue than any other book of the Bible. In fact, without headings to distinguish who is speaking, it would be difficult for the reader to know. This method of recording is so unique in God's word that it, in itself, is a contributing factor to the misunderstandings about the events in the story. The New Testament, with the exception of the gospels, mostly consists of letters written by church leaders for instruction in the truths of God. With the New Testament being in such a take-it-as-you-read-it layout, it is not difficult to see how readers could mistakenly utilize similar methods to interpret the book of Job. Any suggestion that Job should be viewed differently than other scripture is greeted with suspicion because there is a tendency, as God's children, to defend the words of our heavenly Father.

In the story of Job, God has provided an up close and personal account for discerning the truth. The basic emotions that arise in this story are so close to the human heart that I believe God wanted us to experience the raw feelings of the participants. In essence, God is saying, "You are not alone; others have experienced the same pain and confusion." God is compassionate toward His children. God loves Job and all of us <u>who might experience similar confusion</u> and He does not want us to lose hope. *"For whatever things were written before were written for our learning, that we through the patience and comfort of the Scriptures might have hope"* (Romans 15:4).

WHY IS THIS LOVE LETTER UNDER ATTACK?

It is only at the end of the story that Job arrives at his intended destination: <u>the truth of what God is really like</u>.

It is very important to realize that the story of Job is dynamic, with the heart of the main character changing as we are reading. Job is taking a journey throughout this story, but it is only at the end of the story that Job arrives at his intended destination: <u>the truth of what God is really like</u>. The book of Job is the account of one man's heart being suddenly exposed by the fire of oppression. Because of the circumstances of the fallen world that we live in, each of us will experience similar feelings. Hopefully, our situation will never be as extreme as Job's.

I thank God for how willing He is to display the raw emotions of the human heart for our instruction. God has never been reluctant to reveal the character of even His most beloved followers. The book of Job exposes the human heart; the place of our core beliefs. *"For as he thinks in his heart so is he"* (Proverbs 23:7a). In Job we see exactly how one of God's followers is feeling as he lives through great tragedy. As we study the book further, I hope that any fears that have surrounded this wonderful story will be replaced with an appreciation of how our God is trying to communicate with all of us through this narrative.

How much of the book of Job can be used to establish doctrine?

Most of the content in the book of Job is either refuted by God or retracted by Job himself once he understands the true character of God. A very critical question is this: How much of the book of Job can be used to establish doctrine? I will briefly explain why, in my opinion, much of this book cannot be used for that purpose. I am not implying that there is anything wrong with the word of God. My point is, as mostly recorded dialogue, we must be cautious as to what parts of the book we are using for doctrine.

Let me explain with a simple analogy. Imagine a man who was a male chauvinist who had demeaned women most of his life. What if late in life he realizes how foolish he has been and openly confesses his misjudgment of women. Would it be correct to take comments from his earlier views about women as statements of absolute truth? That seems ludicrous, doesn't it? Yet, that is exactly what is done with the words of Job, even though Job openly confesses at the end of the book that he was talking about things that he did not understand. In Job 42:3, Job admits this to God, *"You asked, 'Who is this who hides counsel without knowledge?' Therefore I have uttered <u>what I did not understand</u>, Things too wonderful for me, which <u>I did not know</u>."* Simply put, prior to his receiving an accurate understanding of God, the words of Job are not usable to establish doctrine because he later admits that his earlier statements were incorrect. However, that does not take away from the fact that we have an accurate record of Job's struggle to understand while going through extreme difficulty.

The book of Job is a back stage pass to observe someone dealing with the deceptions of the human heart and how those deceptions lead to erroneous conclusions about the character of God.

This record of Job's struggle to understand what was happening to him openly exposes the deceptiveness of the human heart. *"The heart is <u>deceitful</u> above all things, And desperately wicked: Who can know it? I, the LORD, search the heart, I test the mind, Even to give every man according to his ways, According to the fruit of his doings"* (Jeremiah 17:9-10). The word <u>de-</u>

WHY IS THIS LOVE LETTER UNDER ATTACK?

<u>ceitful</u>[1] means tracked, this is similar to a path which has gotten that way by constant use. Our hearts are prone to take familiar repetitive paths of deception, rather than the more difficult path of facing the truth. In short, it is easier for our hearts to believe a familiar lie than to accept the truth. The book of Job is a back stage pass to observe someone dealing with the deceptions of the human heart and how those deceptions lead to erroneous conclusions about the character of God.

God refutes the words of Job's three friends Himself, and their soliloquies comprise a large part of the book. Job 42:7, *"...The Lord said to Eliphaz the Temanite, 'My wrath is aroused against <u>you and your two friends</u>, for you <u>have not spoken of me what is right</u>, as My servant Job has.'"* I will not avoid the last phrase in that verse, but will address it later in this book. For now, it is absolutely clear that God is saying that the statements of Job's three friends are incorrect.

If Job has retracted his statements and God has refuted the statements of Job's three friends, then what sections of the book are usable for establishing doctrine? Of course, the words of God are truthful; and also the words of Elihu, a younger man who speaks later in the story, are never refuted. Other than these limited areas, we must be very cautious as to what doctrine we try to establish from the book of Job. It would be advantageous to verify any statements in these sections with corroborating evidence in God's word.

I believe it would be wiser to read these portions of the book as a diary of recorded events detailing the feelings and opinions of the participants. None of us takes the opinions of everyone as

---

[1]Any definition of a word from scripture throughout this book is defined from the original Hebrew or Greek language unless otherwise stated.

absolute truth. As Christians, we evaluate people's words based on their character and how their words align with the full counsel of God's word. **It is no different with Job, Elihu, or Job's three friends. We must assess their words by how they line up with the truth contained in the remainder of the word of God.** It is important to not make the serious mistake of taking everyone's words in the book of Job as representing the heart of God. This is a chronicle of actual events which contains all of the opinions of the people involved, irrespective of the accuracy of their understanding. We absolutely must use scripture to corroborate the testimony of anyone in the book of Job. Failure to take this simple precautionary step has caused many doctrinal errors to be formulated from this part of God's word.

Why are we prone to doubt God's goodness?

For a moment let's look back at the serpent's tempting of Eve in the Garden of Eden. He first said that she would not surely die; an attack on the character of God which implied that God had lied. Next, he told Eve that in the day she ate the fruit she would be like God. This was an attack on God's motives which implied that He had been withholding something from man. Therefore, it is easy to see that the ulterior motive behind the attacks was to undermine the character of God.

We need to take an assessment of what Adam and Eve's world was like before sin. They lived in a perfect world, within a perfect environment, within a perfect marriage. There was neither sin nor anything negative. Yet, even in this perfect environment, it was not difficult for them to doubt the character of God. This is despite the fact that they conversed with God daily and He had exhibited no reason for them to question His goodness. Even in perfect man, we see the tendency to doubt the goodness of God.

WHY IS THIS LOVE LETTER UNDER ATTACK?

We need to take an assessment of our world at present. We live in a fallen world full of the results of sin, including the fear of our imminent death. We must be constantly vigilant, looking for the lies of the devil as we take captive the thoughts that come through our minds (2 Corinthians 10:5). If, like Adam and Eve, we possess a tendency to doubt God's goodness and we add to this the multiplied negative experiences of a lifetime, we are even more prone to question God's character than Adam and Eve.

How can this tendency to doubt God's goodness be explained? My simple explanation is that God is so good it is difficult for us to comprehend the depth of His goodness. In 1 Corinthians 13:5 it says that love does not seek its own. By implication, this means that God is never seeking what is in His Own interest, but is literally always looking out for the interests of others. It has always been, and apparently still is, difficult to comprehend a Being that is this selfless.

What is Satan's Strategy?

The origin of most false doctrine from the book of Job comes from us viewing ourselves from a lower standard of worth than God's image of us.

I once asked God an innocent question; "God, why am I understanding so much more than in the past?" I heard in my spirit, "You are losing your self-image." I think God meant I was losing my former self-image and was now beginning to view myself from His perspective. Although I had been a Christian for decades, I was just starting to see myself from God's view point. The origin of most false doctrine from the book of Job comes from us viewing ourselves from a lower standard of worth than God's image of us. Our devalued self-worth creates a distorted view of how God relates to us. This false image in our hearts leads us to misinterpret the events in the story of Job. Our worth has been established by the price that was paid to restore our relationship with God: the life of Jesus Christ. People who do not understand their worth use the book of Job to defend a distorted image of their heavenly Father.

If Satan can distort our understanding of God and the value He places on each one of us, then our defense of God will come from this place of inaccurate understanding. It is crucial that we realize the primary goal of the deceptive strategies utilized against the book of Job is that of corrupting our "knowledge of God". 2 Corinthians 10: 4-5 says, *"For the weapons of our warfare are not carnal but mighty in God for pulling down strongholds, casting down arguments and every high thing that exalts itself <u>against the knowledge of God</u>, bringing every thought into captivity to the obedience of Christ."* The focus of Satan's deceptions is one single target: our knowledge of God. With an accurate understanding of how much God loves us we will no longer be vulnerable to Satan's deceptions.

The effectiveness of Satan's deceptions is evidenced by the erroneous doctrines that have arisen from the book of Job. He has been successful, in part, because of our difficulty in grasping the goodness of God. I believe that Job is Satan's favorite book of the Bible for two reasons. One, Satan is a very pompous creature and this is one of the few places where He is mentioned by name in the word of God. Second, this is a book which Satan has been able to manipulate to his advantage more than any other book of the Bible.

Job is a book full of material perfect for Satan's deceptive arguments against the knowledge of God's love.

WHY IS THIS LOVE LETTER UNDER ATTACK?

Satan's most effective tactic to deceive us is by sowing a lie along the natural path of our human reasoning. However, the Bible is not a book to be understood by human reasoning, but by revelation from the Spirit of God. God's thoughts are filled with how much He loves us, but Job is a book full of material perfect for Satan's deceptive arguments against the knowledge of God's love. At the very heart of the book of Job is the core question: "Can I trust God?" Since "the knowledge of God" is Satan's focus of attack, it is not hard to see why he would manipulate our understanding of God by using the book of Job. I believe Satan revels in the destructive doctrines of God's character that have been birthed out of the book of Job.

How is man honored by God?

For months I was led by God to say this prayer many times a day; "Thank You, God, for you have blessed me and prospered me in every way. I praise You because I am fearfully and wonderfully made, and that my soul knows full well." That last part is a partial quote of Psalms 139:14, "*I will praise You, for I am fearfully and wonderfully made; Marvelous are Your works, And that my soul knows very well.*" Each time I would say it, I became more focused upon the phrase "fearfully and wonderfully made", but what does that mean?

> ***In all of creation, man alone was fashioned after an existing image.***

The word fearfully means to fear; morally, to revere. God is clearly saying that He has placed a reverence or a fearful respect upon mankind. This can help explain the moral horror we feel when we see someone being abused. Any mental or physical abuse is in stark contrast to the honor that God has given mankind. The word <u>wonderfully</u> means to distinguish, put a difference, show marvelous, or separate. There is a distinct difference or separation between mankind and everything else that God created. Mankind is created in the likeness of another image: the image of God. In all of creation, man alone was fashioned after an existing image.

If people are being devalued, whatever is taking place is not of God.

Sometimes people over-exaggerate their feelings for animals, even to the point of laying down their lives for them. This only serves to lower God's exalted position for mankind. There is nothing in all of creation that even comes close to the marvelous wonder of a human being. Man is unique because he is fearfully and wonderfully made. This is why the devil will shame, undermine, devalue, or degrade people any way he can. If people are being devalued, whatever is taking place is not of God.

God honored mankind by placing him above everything else which He made. *"What is man that You are mindful of him, And the son of man that You visit him? For You have made him a little lower than the angels, And <u>You have crowned him with glory and honor</u>. <u>You have made him to have dominion over the works of Your hands</u>; <u>You have put all things under his feet</u>, All sheep and oxen—Even the beasts of the field, The birds of the air, And the fish of the sea That pass through the paths of the seas"* (Psalms 8:4-8). It is important to understand the position of respect and honor that God bestowed upon His greatest creation: mankind. The foundation of our understanding of our current world must be grounded in God's honor of mankind prior to man's rebellion in the Garden of Eden. **Understanding the exalted position in which God placed mankind is crucial to understanding the events that now transpire in our world.**

CHAPTER 2

WHY IS THE MEANING OF "SOVEREIGNTY" A TARGET?

Who is responsible for distorting the concept of sovereignty?

Satan has sown lies in our hearts, causing us to embrace a non-relational version of God. One method he uses from the book of Job to achieve this disconnection from God is the misrepresentation of the concept of "sovereignty". A <u>sovereign</u>, as defined by Webster, is one who possesses supreme power, or one who exercises supreme authority; it is used in reference to the rule of a king, called a sovereign. Satan's distorted version of sovereignty implies that because God is "<u>The</u> Sovereign" then nothing happens which He does not cause to happen. This leads to the conclusion that everything which happens is part of God's plan. The implication is that God is responsible for both good and bad actions. Satan's distortion of the meaning of sovereignty leads to some very inaccurate conclusions about the character of God.

If we believe a God of love is responsible for both good and bad events, then if a person were in a car wreck we must conclude that God caused the wreck. Logically, how could this be possible? Why would God, who is Love, (1 John 4:16) hurt His child? This distorted logic does not line up with the character of God which we see in Christ. Something seems confused and twisted about the concept of a loving heavenly Father purposely doing us harm. Sounds like the lie of an enemy whose only weapon is deception.

Satan's perverted version of sovereignty corresponds perfectly with our tendency to doubt God's goodness. Satan's contrived schizophrenic god is completely opposite to the God of Malachi 3:6a Who never changes, *"For I am the Lord, I do not change."* Most all discussions about Job will focus on this false understanding of sovereignty. Satan has, for the most part, been able to derail God's original purpose for recording the story of Job.

Blaming is just one way of providing a temporary reprieve for our anxious heart, but it can never bring the true rest God desires for us.

This false sovereignty is particularly attractive to our sin nature because it gives us the opportunity to blame somebody. We want to make sense of the evil in our fallen world, so we feel compelled to pin the blame on someone. True rest cannot be achieved by blaming others. Blaming is just one way of providing a temporary reprieve for our anxious heart, but it can never bring the true rest God desires for us. We cannot allow our desire for answers and our need for security in the midst of life's chaos to become a substitute for our true need: a personal relationship with God.

How is sovereignty used to divide us?

To accurately understand the attempt to distort sovereignty, we must understand the driving motives of our mutual enemy, the devil. James 3:16 says, *"For where <u>envy</u> and self-seeking exist, <u>confusion</u> and every evil thing are there."* Satan <u>envies</u> our position as children of God and co-heirs with Christ. He will attempt, at all costs, to <u>confuse</u> our understanding of God. Satan is greatly concerned that we will learn how important we are to

Why is the Meaning of "Sovereignty" a Target?

God. For Satan's agenda to be successful, it is critical that we never find out how much God loves us.

The false understanding of sovereignty is, by far, the most controversial doctrine arising from the book of Job. Even if we disagree on the topic of sovereignty, let us hold fast to the truth that we are all children with the same heavenly Father. Our Daddy is so big He does not actually need us to defend Him. The reason the topic of God's sovereignty can provoke such violent opposition is because it comes against the strongholds of deceptions the enemy has already sown into our hearts. These deceptions are a targeted attack against our understanding of our mutual heavenly Father. They were sown by the devil who would like nothing more than to have God's children fighting among themselves. The church's in-fighting over these lies has failed to display the character of Christ. As a result, this has turned many away from the church. No one wants to join a dysfunctional family!

Not only do Satan's tactics cause us to fight each other, they can also cause those of us who know God to hopelessly languish in our pursuit of Him. We can develop this "it doesn't really matter" attitude which will render us useless in our objective of bringing others into a personal relationship with God. Both in-fighting and hopelessness are accomplished by Satan through the false understanding of sovereignty. It is absolutely crucial in this spiritual war that we be aware of the schemes of our enemy and take precautionary measures against his attacks. Part of Satan's agenda is to promote a misunderstanding of the meaning of sovereignty in the minds of those in the body of Christ

Anyone who desires to effectively advance the kingdom of God must be aware of the enemy at all times.

I have been explaining what might happen in our hearts as we study the book of Job. This is not wasted time; it is a time of basic training in awareness. Gideon's final three hundred soldiers were chosen by God based on their vigilant watch for the enemy during a time of peace (Judges 7:5-7). Anyone who desires to effectively advance the kingdom of God must be aware of the enemy at all times. Job himself is evidence of someone who was grossly unaware of Satan's attacks. We are engaged in a war. The battles are for our hearts, and we must be prepared to fight our common enemy. Our true understanding of God is absolutely essential to fight a winning war. It is time to take back what has been stolen from the body of Christ. <u>The word of God is ours to enjoy, not Satan's to distort</u>.

Why did God allow it?

Many times the questions we have about Job's story are so intense because they mirror the same questions we have about events that take place in our own lives: One of those questions is: "Why did God <u>allow</u> it?" When we ask this question we are making the huge assumption that God can intervene the way we have imagined He should when bad events happen in our lives. I would like to propose that this is not possible. God has not ordered the universe by our perception of what He "should" do. He has ordered the universe by His word. *"Who being the brightness of His glory and the express image of His person, and <u>upholding all things by the word of His power</u>, when He had by Himself purged our sins, sat down at the right hand of the Majesty on high"* (Hebrews 1:3). God has chosen to use His word as the means of transmitting and sustaining His power.

The unchanging integrity of God and His word, have far reaching affects.

Why is the Meaning of "Sovereignty" a Target?

When God makes a decision, He seals the finality of that decision by His word which is backed by His power to enforce it. God is always true to His word no matter the cost. Part of the integrity of God is that He does not change (Malachi 3:6a). James 1:17 makes it clear that there is not even the slightest variation in God's character, *"Every good gift and every perfect gift is from above, and comes down from the Father of lights, <u>with whom there is no variation or shadow of turning</u>."* Because God cannot change this means His word cannot change. The unchanging integrity of God and His word have far reaching affects.

All things exist and are held together by the word of God. Genesis chapter 1 gives us a record of what God said, followed immediately by what He had spoken coming into existence. Jesus is God's Word in the flesh, *"And the Word became flesh and dwelt among us, and we beheld His glory, the glory as of the only begotten of the Father, full of grace and truth"* (John 1:14). No word or action of Jesus Christ can ever change because he is the integrity of God Himself; Jesus is the Word of God. Jesus (the Word of God) established all of creation. *"For <u>by Him (Jesus) all things were created</u> that are in heaven and that are on earth, visible and invisible, whether thrones or dominions or principalities or powers. <u>All things were created through Him and for Him</u>. And He is before all things, and in Him all things consist"* (Colossians 1:16-17).

The assumption that God can randomly intervene, whenever He so chooses, is actually in opposition to God's word.

It would be utterly foolish to believe God could go against His own word because the integrity of God's word is what upholds all things (Hebrews 1:3). The assumption that God can randomly intervene, whenever He so chooses, is actually in opposition to God's word. This assumption cunningly implies that God is able to go against His own word, while the truth is that this will never happen. Here is a simple example: *"Then God said 'let there be light'; and there was light"* (Genesis 1:3). Therefore, there will always be light. *"My covenant I will not break, Nor alter the word that has gone out of My lips."* (Psalms 89:34). Because God can never violate His word, it is very important to know exactly what He has said. God's word <u>cannot</u> fail!

The first words that God ever spoke to man are recorded in Genesis 1:28, *"Then God blessed them, and God said to them, 'Be fruitful and multiply; fill the earth and subdue it; have dominion over the fish of the sea, over the birds of the air, and over every living thing that moves on the earth'."* The word <u>dominion</u> here means to subjugate, prevail against, reign, or rule. By God's Own word He gave man authority over the earth. Knowing the integrity of God leads us to the understanding that He will <u>never</u> violate this word which gave us our authority. **Most of the time God is not intervening because He gave us the authority in that area and to intervene would violate His word which gave us that authority.** The real problem is this: <u>we do not believe we have the authority that He gave us</u>. As we begin to get a deeper revelation of how much God loves us it will not only alleviate the fears that surround the subject of His sovereignty, but it will renew our minds to the authority He has given us.

Why didn't God intervene?

The question, "Why didn't God intervene?" is the same as, "Why did God allow it?" The difference is that one is expecting God to be passive (allow it) while the other is expecting God to be active (intervene). Both questions have the hidden assumption that God can control events whenever He chooses. It is not that God is unable to be actively involved in situations, it is that His <u>Self-imposed</u> boundaries <u>must</u> stop at the point where He would be required to violate the integrity of His Own word. God cannot break His word!

Without our agreement, God would be violating His own word which gave us our authority.

God can be extremely supernatural in leading us toward the right decision, but He will neither violate His word nor impose His will on us. He moved a star for the wise men to follow to the place of Jesus's birth, but He did not make them follow the star. The wise men had to make a free will choice to follow the leading of the star. Just as God needed the rod and words of Moses to accomplish His will for the Hebrews, he needs the agreement of our authority before He can act on our behalf. Without our agreement, God would be violating His own word which gave us our authority. <u>A true understanding of sovereignty does not cause me to be angry at God, but it causes me to reverence God and the integrity of His Word</u>. This knowledge bolsters my faith because I know if God has spoken anything, then that is the way it has to be, without exception.

What about the filter of God's will?

I recently heard of someone making this statement, "Nothing happens unless it is filtered through the will of God. "I feel the need to address this before we go further. Satan's lies are very unoriginal and only tend to vary slightly. This one is nothing more than another version of, "Nothing happens unless God allows it." This slightly different statement is another attempt to place God into a false "all-controlling-Sovereign" position so that He will be blamed for evil. Remember, because this is not a direct attack on the character of God, it does not seem as dangerous. But, if we believe it, it will have the same effect.

CAN I TRUST GOD

Why do bad things happen to good people?

One of the most difficult situations for us to handle is witnessing a tragedy happen to someone that we care about. In our love and concern there is one overwhelming thought, "They do not deserve this!" In those moments we are sensing something we know on a heart level: there should be justice. One thing we know for sure, what is happening to our loved one is not just. I am not going to give you some trite nonsensical answer like what happened was for their good, or God had a bigger plan. And if they have died because of this tragedy, I will never tell you that God took them because He needed them more. The feelings these tragedies evoke are as truthful and right as any feelings could ever be true and right. They did not deserve it and it was not just. It was horrible and people who tell us otherwise are not only naïve, they are deceived.

Justice, as we know it should be, seems almost elusive in this world. This is just one example of the many scenarios of injustice that take place in our world every single day: a woman can be raped and become pregnant. If the attacker is caught and punished, it most likely will not be for long. The victim on the other hand is left not only with the trauma of the event, but with major life-changing decisions. She may choose to end the life of her own child or go through nine months of labor and delivery only to give the child away accompanied with possible feelings of regret. Or she could choose to keep the child and face the difficult responsibility of unplanned parenthood. The victim never should have had the anguish of making any of those decisions, yet all of this unwarranted anxiety was forced upon her. The truth is undeniable: this is not right, this is not fair, this is not just, and she did not deserve it.

Why is the Meaning of "Sovereignty" a Target?

We can become angry at injustice because no wrong was ever meant to happen.

We are now getting to the heart of our frustrations. Why do bad things happen to good people? The hidden assumption in this question is that bad things should happen to bad people while only good things should happen to good people. The reality is that good and bad events happen to us all. But, why is it this way when we all know that it should not be? Whether we call it our heart, our spirit, or our inner man, we all seem to know that this is not the way it was meant to be. The truth is we are correct; it ought to be closer to the way our heart perceives that it should. We can become angry at injustice because no wrong was ever meant to happen. All tragedies should never have taken place! So, the real frustrating question is this: Why does so much bad happen if it is not supposed to happen?

Bad things happen every day that are not the will of God. If we believe that this is not true, then we must come to the conclusion that we worship a very sick and twisted God. This lie is exactly what Satan would like for us to believe. The problems that affect mankind are not the result of God having a twisted character. They are the result of mankind being entrusted with authority on earth. By partaking of the tree of the knowledge of good and evil, the rebellion of Adam and Eve brought with it the enticing desires which lead the free will of many to choose evil and not good. Satan is more than willing to use these enticements, along with his lies, to draw people toward wrong decisions. Mankind's continued obedience to God's command in the Garden of Eden would have avoided all of this. Now, the daily ramifications of evil choices are simply a fact of our fallen world.

To truly change the world for good we must use our influence to inspire and encourage others to come into a personal relationship with God which will result in submission to His Lordship. Once in this relationship, we are able to be led by God so He can once again accomplish His loving will on the earth as it was in the beginning. As God's ambassadors, His desire is that we believe in His words which are able to overcome the evil on this earth.

The authority we have been given in Christ is much more powerful than most of us realize. Our authority is activated by faith in God and is apparently unlimited. *"So Jesus answered and said to them, 'Have faith in God. For assuredly, I say to you, whoever says to this mountain, 'Be removed and be cast into the sea,' and does not doubt in his heart, but believes that those things he says will be done, he will have whatever he says. Therefore I say to you, whatever things you ask when you pray, believe that you receive them, and you will have them'"* (Mark 11:22-24). I have witnessed and heard of many awesome exploits that have been done through someone who believed in the word of God. I expect to see many more in the future as those who are submitted to the Lordship of Christ continue to grow in the knowledge of God's love for them.

Why do we underestimate the effects of our rebellion?

God did not send Jesus to die on the cross to take care of a minor problem.

Lenard Cohen in his famous song "Halleluiah"[A] has a line that goes like this, "the minor fall and the major lift." Based on the context of the song, I believe this is a reference to the "major lift" (the redemption of mankind through Christ's work on the cross) being overdone in comparison with the "minor fall" (mankind's rebellion against God). Nothing could be fur-

Why is the Meaning of "Sovereignty" a Target?

ther from the truth. Most of us, like Mr. Cohen, have underestimated the size of the solution needed to solve the problem of man's rebellion. We have underestimated the level of authority God originally delegated to mankind and the corresponding ramifications.

God did not send Jesus to die on the cross to take care of a <u>minor</u> problem. No parent would agree to willingly sacrifice his/her only son if there was another way. **A critical misunderstanding of man's rebellion against God in the Garden of Eden has been to overlook the elevated position of authority mankind held when they rebelled.** The higher the position of authority, the more damage is caused when someone destroys the integrity of the authority entrusted to them.

Sadly, we do not have to look far in the church to see this principle clearly demonstrated. There have been far too many church leaders who have succumbed to personal temptation only to find that their sin had a far reaching effect, damaging the body of Christ as a whole. We all have a tendency to underestimate the influence we have on others. As Christians, we are not islands unto ourselves; we are interconnected parts of the body of Christ. *"For as the body is one and has many members, but all the members of that one body, being many, are one body, so also is Christ. For by one Spirit we were all baptized into one body--whether Jews or Greeks, whether slaves or free--and have all been made to drink into one Spirit"* (1 Corinthians 12:12-13). God has given each of us authority and this authority causes us to have influence over others. The delegation of authority always brings with it the ability to influence others for good as well as influence them for evil.

Adam and Eve were given authority over all of the earth along with the authority to reproduce and thereby multiply the human race (Genesis 1:28). It is very clear that Adam and Eve were God's appointed and delegated authority over all of the earth. Therefore, their rebellion, through sin, negatively influenced everything under their authority. Adam and Eve's choice of evil provided that choice to their offspring, the entire human race. Now, not only do Adam and Eve's descendants have the ability to reproduce evil, they also lack the understanding of their own authority and have an obscured view of the God Who gave them their authority.

God's command to not eat from the tree of the knowledge of good and evil (Genesis 2:17) was not given as a test to determine Adam and Eve's ability to resist temptation. *"Let no one say when he is tempted, 'I am tempted by God'; for God cannot be tempted by evil, nor does He Himself tempt anyone"* (James 1:13). God's command originated from the protecting heart of a loving heavenly Father. God knew that without the knowledge of good and evil, mankind would have only reproduced from His heart. Since God is love (1 John 4:16) then only good would have been reproduced on the earth. Believing the serpent's lies about God's motives caused man to step outside the safety of God's protection. This opened the door for the dangers of evil to impact the human race.

The human race, apart from the knowledge of God's love, is not progressing morally.

We live in a world which has experienced thousands of years of evil. Recent events reported on the news have displayed extreme examples of human brutality, such as severing the head from the body and even burning someone alive. These only serve to remind us that the human race, apart from the knowledge of God's love, is not progressing morally. As we advance in technical achievements, the contrast of the increase of human

Why is the Meaning of "Sovereignty" a Target?

depravity only serves to remind us that mental achievements never ensure the needed moral change which our world is lacking. Only love can make this world what it was intended to be, and true love can only flourish under the authority of God which man continues to rebel against.

Even in the church, many believers think they can achieve the plans of God without being under His authority, but that very rebellion is the root of the catastrophe we find ourselves in today. Jesus's words on this go directly to the point, *"But why do you call Me 'Lord, Lord,' and not do the things which I say? Whoever comes to Me, and hears My sayings and does them, I will show you whom he is like: He is like a man building a house, who dug deep and laid the foundation on the rock. And when the flood arose, the stream beat vehemently against that house, and could not shake it, for it was founded on the rock. But he who heard and did nothing is like a man who built a house on the earth without a foundation, against which the stream beat vehemently; and immediately it fell. And the ruin of that house was great"* (Luke 6:46-49). Persons who are not submitted to the God of love will come to ruin. Like Adam and Eve, they will succumb to the influences of evil because they have chosen to be outside of the authority of God.

[A] Various Positions, 1984

CHAPTER 3

WHY DO WE LONG TO TRUST GOD?

Where did Job's desire for rest come from?

We were created to live in an environment of dependence not independence.

Sometimes, because of familiarity, we can accept our circumstances as being normal when, in actuality, they are not. We are living in a world that has been thrown into chaos by the effects of sin, a world where we feel separated from God. It is very important to understand that we were not created to live in this fallen world, but in a different world altogether. We were created to live in a world without the effects of sin. Consider the implications of this amazing truth: the bad circumstances of our lives were never meant to happen! Our negative experiences are not even the worst consequence of man's rebellion. The most severe consequence is the separation that we feel from God.

Man's rebellion brought independence, but we were created to live in an environment of dependence not independence. Man was created to live in a restful, trusting, dependent relationship with God. This relationship, founded upon trust, provided the safe place needed to allow Adam and Eve to push through any obstacle without fear. Man's trust in God was vital to the fulfillment of their assignment. *"Then God blessed them, and God said to them, 'Be fruitful and multiply; fill the earth and subdue it; have dominion over the fish of the sea, over the birds of the air, and over every living thing that moves on the earth'"* (Genesis 1:28).

The security provided by being able to rest in the total assurance of God's love eradicates all fear. *"There is no fear in love; but perfect love casts out fear, because fear involves torment. But he who fears has not been made perfect in love"* (1 John 4:18). Without the presence of fear, Adam and Eve, along with their descendants, would have been able to experience their full potential through the fulfillment of God's assignment. <u>Just imagine what mankind would have been able to achieve if not a single person had ever been afraid</u>! What if every creative idea had never been discouraged, but only encouraged through a loving relationship? Envision a world where no good thing had ever been resisted!

We all desire legitimate answers for the problems we face in our lives. Only a trusting relationship with God can provide the answers that we are seeking. The way most of us live— questioning, wondering, doubting, and worrying—is not how we were intended to live. In fact, this is not really living at all. Jesus said, *"I have come that they may have <u>life</u>, and that they may have it more abundantly"* (John 10:10b). Jesus made true life available to us by destroying the shame of sin which undermines our dependence upon God. *"Looking unto Jesus, the author and finisher of our faith, who for the joy that was set before Him endured the cross, <u>despising the shame</u>, and has sat down at the right hand of the throne of God"* (Hebrews 12:2). God never intended for us to worry about our lives, but to trust Him for the answers. "Be anxious for nothing, but in everything by prayer and supplication, with thanksgiving, let your requests be made known to God" (Philippians 4:6).

Since most of us have <u>not</u> learned how to trust God, we often develop coping mechanisms to deal with the troubles we are facing. Sometimes we feel like we "deserve" a break. The belief that we are "owed" something because of how difficult our life is can often be an avenue of temptation. Trying to cope with our frustrations can tempt us to over-indulge in any area. For example, we can decide to reward ourselves with excess food because we feel we "deserve" the comfort which food provides. There is nothing wrong with treating ourselves or taking a break. But, it is dangerous when this desire is used to replace our legitimate need for trusting God. This is like using a Band-Aid on a knife wound; it is never going to adequately stop the bleeding.

We must first firmly establish that God is not the one causing our problems before we will ever be able to trust Him.

In many situations where we over-indulge we are trying to fill our legitimate need for a trusting relationship with God with a pathetic earthly substitute. We are taking the insecurity which we have over the unpredictability in our lives and using that fear to justify our actions. The problem is that these substitutes will never give us relief from the anxiety we are facing. **We need the security of knowing that we can absolutely trust God.** But, how are we going to trust God if we believe He is the source of our troubles? It must first be firmly established that God is not the one causing our problems before we will ever be able to trust Him.

This might surprise you, but <u>our anger over the consequences of sin is justified</u>. "Be angry, and do not sin" (Ephesians 4:26a). The problem does not lie in our anger; the problem lies in the misdirection of our anger. Satan has used the book of Job to devise a clever distortion of the concept of sovereignty. Satan's misappropriation of the true meaning of sovereignty ultimately causes our anger over the effects of sin to be misdirected toward God. The irony is that Satan gets off scot free when he was the one who actually initiated man's temptation and introduced sin into the world. **I believe the book of Job was written to expose**

our misdirected anger and frustration. Our heavenly Father, Who loves us beyond comprehension intends to lead us to the only true place of rest: a trusting relationship with Him. The book of Job gives us invaluable insight into the root of our anger. Isn't it ironic that the most heated debates over God's word center around the perceived controversies in the book of Job?

Job had developed his own system of coping with his fears of uncertainty. Job's method of coping was not overindulging his flesh, <u>but trusting in his own works</u>. Job's trust in himself was a pathetic substitute for what he really needed which was the knowledge that He could completely trust his heavenly Father. God wanted Job to know He loved him and that He could be trusted. God did not need to be pacified with Job's sacrifices. *"For I desire mercy and not sacrifice, and the knowledge of God more than burnt offerings"* (Hosea 6:6).

The book of Job is often avoided by teachers because of the unspoken fear of the resulting repercussions. The amount of controversy surrounding the book of Job is itself proof of the value to be found in its pages. Satan does not waste his time on targets of little value. If you believe the book of Job is irrelevant, I hope you will allow me the opportunity to prove otherwise. I believe God's revelations from this part of His word will have a profound impact on your personal relationship with Him.

What is wrong with wanting life to be easy?

Job is searching for the same security most of us are, though we may not realize it. Job reveals what he is looking for by his reaction when the opposite comes to pass. *"For the thing I greatly feared has come upon me, and what I dreaded has happened to me. <u>I am not at ease, nor am I quiet; I have no rest</u>, for trouble* *comes"* (Job 3:25-26). Here is what Job was after: he wanted life to be easy. Right now that may not seem important, but I am going to demonstrate to you how this basic human desire is a driving influence in our lives. For those of you who think you are not pursuing ease and rest, I have a couple of examples that may help you to re-think your position.

The first thought of anyone who has a vehicle with a persistent, reoccurring mechanical problem is: "I hope nothing goes wrong with the car today!" We are thinking this way because we desire for things to go well; we want life to be easy and free of trouble. This is how we all are predisposed to think and I will show you that we were created to think this way. Even though this is a basic human desire, it can inadvertently become a driving motivator in our lives which, if not recognized, can become a very serious problem.

When I speak before a group I ask them to imagine an extremely wealthy person and to picture him/her involved in some activity. It can be absolutely anything. They might visualize someone golfing, sailing, or flying in a private jet. What I have found consistent anywhere I have done this exercise is that the imagined activity is never a form of work. Although I am sure that many wealthy people did not acquire their wealth without hard work, no one imagines them working. Almost, without exception, everyone in the audience imagines someone involved in a leisure activity. I personally pictured someone sipping a drink while yachting on the Mediterranean Sea. We tend to picture someone resting because that is what we desire for ourselves: rest. I have yet to see anyone picture this wealthy person at a board meeting.

Whether we realize it or not, we do not actually desire to be rich. We desire the ease of life which money is able to provide.

If I said I was giving someone the choice of millions of dollars or the ability to do whatever they wanted without having to worry about money for the rest of their life, most people would take the second option. This is because, like Job, we all desire ease and rest, and that is why I believe God used him as our example.

You were not created to be fulfilled by rest, but by life and that life is in God.

Enjoying ease and rest is not wrong, unless we desire this rest as a substitute for trusting God. We were not created to be fulfilled by rest, but by life and that life is in God. *"In Him was life, and the life was the light of men"* (John 1:4). If we are seeking rest as a substitute for God, that is idolatry and God hates idolatry, not because He is egotistical, but because He knows it is a poor substitute for true life which can only be found in Him. We are commanded in Matthew 6:33, *"But seek first the kingdom of God and His righteousness, and all these things shall be added to you."* One of our biggest desires is peace and rest, but God's genuine peace only comes as we pursue Him. *"You will keep him in perfect peace, whose mind is stayed on You, because he trusts in You."* (Isaiah 26:3a).

How can tragedy affect us?

I once attended a church where I was faced with a situation I wish I had handled differently. I was attending a Sunday School Class that immediately preceded the Sunday Morning Worship Service. The teacher taught the class from a misunderstanding of God's sovereignty. He believed that God was responsible for every action that takes place. I later learned that the gentleman who taught the class had had a tragedy occur in his life. Someone he loved had died at a young age.

Why Do We Long to Trust God?

Many people who have been wounded in a relationship of the heart tend to gravitate toward a misunderstanding of God's absolute sovereignty. The hurt of losing someone we are close to can lead to anger, and in our anger is the yearning for someone to be accountable for our loss. These people are easily recognized by their defensive response when it is mentioned that something is not God's fault.

As the gentleman taught the class, I would make a comment like, "Well, that doesn't seem right, God is good." At that point his defenses would go up, and this process just began to escalate. It got to the point where we stayed and argued after class through an entire worship service. Later an associate pastor was sent to meet with me and explain the church's position on some of the topics we had been discussing. I later discovered that the associate pastor had a long term medical condition. This may also lead someone to embrace a misunderstanding of the sovereignty of God. At that meeting I was presented with what they felt was their church's position on God's sovereignty. There were eight stated positions on topics that would have been in question concerning God's sovereignty: <u>six out of the eight positions came from the book of Job</u>. I kept that paper for years but regrettably, later lost it. It was one of the most amazing positional statements I have ever seen. When I hear lies about how <u>un</u>important writing about the book of Job is, I remember that paper.

Reading Job's Story

I have included Job chapters one through three here because it will be very helpful for us to have the story fresh on our minds as we proceed further.

CAN I TRUST GOD

Job - Chapter 1

1 "There was a man in the land of Uz, whose name was Job; and that man was blameless and upright, and one who feared God and shunned evil. 2 And seven sons and three daughters were born to him. 3 Also, his possessions were seven thousand sheep, three thousand camels, five hundred yoke of oxen, five hundred female donkeys, and a very large household, so that this man was the greatest of all the people of the East.

4 "And his sons would go and feast in their houses, each on his appointed day, and would send and invite their three sisters to eat and drink with them. 5 So it was, when the days of feasting had run their course, that Job would send and sanctify them, and he would rise early in the morning and offer burnt offerings according to the number of them all. For Job said, 'It may be that my sons have sinned and cursed God in their hearts.' Thus Job did regularly.

6 "Now there was a day when the sons of God came to present themselves before the Lord, and Satan also came among them. 7 And the Lord said to Satan, 'From where do you come?' So Satan answered the Lord and said, 'From going to and fro on the earth, and from walking back and forth on it.' 8 Then the Lord said to Satan, 'Have you considered My servant Job, that there is none like him on the earth, a blameless and upright man, one who fears God and shuns evil'?

9 "So Satan answered the Lord and said, 'Does Job fear God for nothing? 10 Have You not made a hedge around him, around his household, and around all that he has on

every side? You have blessed the work of his hands, and his possessions have increased in the land. 11 But now, stretch out Your hand and touch all that he has, and he will surely curse You to Your face!' 12 And the Lord said to Satan, 'Behold, all that he has is in your power; only do not lay a hand on his person.' So Satan went out from the presence of the Lord.

13 "Now there was a day when his sons and daughters were eating and drinking wine in their oldest brother's house; 14 and a messenger came to Job and said, 'The oxen were plowing and the donkeys feeding beside them, 15 when the Sabeans raided them and took them away — indeed they have killed the servants with the edge of the sword; and I alone have escaped to tell you'! 16 While he was still speaking, another also came and said, 'The fire of God fell from heaven and burned up the sheep and the servants, and consumed them; and I alone have escaped to tell you'! 17 While he was still speaking, another also came and said, 'The Chaldeans formed three bands, raided the camels and took them away, yes, and killed the servants with the edge of the sword; and I alone have escaped to tell you'!

18 "While he was still speaking, another also came and said, 'Your sons and daughters were eating and drinking wine in their oldest brother's house, 19 and suddenly a great wind came from across the wilderness and struck the four corners of the house, and it fell on the young people, and they are dead; and I alone have escaped to tell you'! 20 Then Job arose, tore his robe, and shaved his head; and he fell to the ground and worshiped. 21 And he said: 'Naked I came from my mother's womb, And naked shall I return there. The Lord gave, and the

Lord has taken away; Blessed be the name of the Lord.' 22 In all this Job did not sin nor charge God with wrong.

Job - Chapter 2

1 "Again there was a day when the sons of God came to present themselves before the Lord, and Satan came also among them to present himself before the Lord. 2 And the Lord said to Satan, 'From where do you come?' Satan answered the Lord and said, 'From going to and fro on the earth, and from walking back and forth on it.' 3 Then the Lord said to Satan, 'Have you considered My servant Job, that there is none like him on the earth, a blameless and upright man, one who fears God and shuns evil? And still he holds fast to his integrity, although you incited Me against him, to destroy him without cause'.

4 "So Satan answered the Lord and said, 'Skin for skin! Yes, all that a man has he will give for his life. 5 But stretch out Your hand now, and touch his bone and his flesh, and he will surely curse You to Your face!' 6 And the Lord said to Satan, 'Behold, he is in your hand, but spare his life.' 7 So Satan went out from the presence of the Lord, and struck Job with painful boils from the sole of his foot to the crown of his head. 8 And he took for himself a potsherd with which to scrape himself while he sat in the midst of the ashes.

9 "Then his wife said to him, 'Do you still hold fast to your integrity? Curse God and die!' 10 But he said to her, 'You speak as one of the foolish women speaks. Shall we indeed accept good from God, and shall we not accept adversity?' In all this Job did not sin with his lips.

Why Do We Long to Trust God?

11 "Now when Job's three friends heard of all this adversity that had come upon him, each one came from his own place — Eliphaz the Temanite, Bildad the Shuhite, and Zophar the Naamathite. For they had made an appointment together to come and mourn with him, and to comfort him. 12 And when they raised their eyes from afar, and did not recognize him, they lifted their voices and wept; and each one tore his robe and sprinkled dust on his head toward heaven. 13 So they sat down with him on the ground seven days and seven nights, and no one spoke a word to him, for they saw that his grief was very great'.

Job - Chapter 3

1 "After this Job opened his mouth and cursed the day of his birth. 2 And Job spoke, and said: 3 'May the day perish on which I was born, And the night in which it was said, 'A male child is conceived'. 4 May that day be darkness; May God above not seek it, Nor the light shine upon it. 5 May darkness and the shadow of death claim it; May a cloud settle on it; May the blackness of the day terrify it. 6 As for that night, may darkness seize it; May it not rejoice among the days of the year, May it not come into the number of the months.

7 "'Oh, may that night be barren! May no joyful shout come into it! 8 May those curse it who curse the day, Those who are ready to arouse Leviathan. 9 May the stars of its morning be dark; May it look for light, but have none, And not see the dawning of the day; 10 Because it did not shut up the doors of my mother's womb, Nor hide sorrow from my eyes. 11 Why did I not die at birth? Why did I not perish when I came from the womb?

12 Why did the knees receive me? Or why the breasts, that I should nurse?

13 "'For now I would have lain still and been quiet, I would have been asleep; Then I would have been at rest 14 With kings and counselors of the earth, Who built ruins for themselves, 15 Or with princes who had gold, Who filled their houses with silver; 16 Or why was I not hidden like a stillborn child, Like infants who never saw light? 17 There the wicked cease from troubling, And there the weary are at rest. 18 There the prisoners rest together; They do not hear the voice of the oppressor. 19 The small and great are there, And the servant is free from his master.

20 "'Why is light given to him who is in misery, And life to the bitter of soul, 21 Who long for death, but it does not come, And search for it more than hidden treasures; 22 Who rejoice exceedingly, And are glad when they can find the grave? 23 Why is light given to a man whose way is hidden, And whom God has hedged in? 24 For my sighing comes before I eat, And my groanings pour out like water. 25 For the thing I greatly feared has come upon me, And what I dreaded has happened to me. 26 I am not at ease, nor am I quiet; I have no rest, for trouble comes.'"

What kind of relationship does Job have with God?

When we take a closer look at Job's relationship with God, there is something dreadfully wrong. Job has been deceived about God's character and this is simple to prove. If we were to put ourselves into Job's situation and we had just lost all our children and everything we owned in a matter of minutes, what would be our instinctive response? Most of us would drop to our knees pleading for God's help. However, in all of his tragedy, Job <u>never</u> asks God for help. This fact alone tells us that there is clearly something fundamentally wrong in Job's relationship with God.

Why does Job not ask God for help? It is because, according to his own words, Job considers God to be the source of his problems. One of the most quoted scriptures in all of the Bible is Job's mistaken accusation against God. *"The LORD gave, <u>and the LORD has taken away</u>; blessed be the name of the LORD"* (Job 1:21b). Did God really kill Job's children? Could this really be the same God Who sent His Son to die on a cross so that anyone who calls on His name can be saved (Romans 10:13); the same God that is not willing that any should perish (2 Peter 3:9)? This does not make sense because it is the wrong conclusion. This is a complete misunderstanding of who is responsible! We have an enemy who seeks to do us harm and his name is Satan. We have a God who loves us enough to sacrifice His only Son for our rescue. He cannot be the one doing us harm. Every war has an enemy and our enemy is not God!

Who wants to pursue a God Who would kill their children?

If someone was beating us up, would we ever stop them to ask for their help to stop the beating? No one would even consider such a thought! In that same way, Job is so sure that God is the One causing his troubles there is no indication that he even considers asking God for help. **How is a relational God supposed to have a relationship with someone who is deceived about His motives?** God has billions of His children living in the same misunderstanding. In Jeremiah 29:13 God makes this proclamation, "And you will seek Me, and find Me, when you search for Me with all your heart." Who wants to pursue a God Who would kill their children? The goal of Satan's deceptions about the character of God is to stop us from pursuing Him.

Why compare Job's relationship with God to David's?

The best way I have found to understand Job's relationship with God is to compare it with David's. I usually do not condone comparison, but when it is used for the Godly purpose of spiritual discernment, it can be very helpful in our understanding of Job. God calls David, *"...a man after His/My Own heart"* (I Samuel 13:14; Acts 13:22); therefore, by God's Own word, David is someone we can look to as a model for relationship with Him. Reading some of David's thoughts and comparing them to Job's will give us valuable insight.

We often see David proclaiming that God is for Him, and God is his deliverer. In Psalms 56:9 he says, *"When I cry out to You, then my enemies will turn back; This I know because **God is for me**"*(emphasis added). Here is a very familiar Psalm of David, *"I will love You, O Lord, my strength. The Lord is my rock and my fortress and my deliverer; my God, my strength, in whom I will trust; my shield and the horn of my salvation, my stronghold. I will call upon the Lord who is worthy to be praised; so shall I be saved from my enemies"* (Psalms 18:1-3). Twenty-one times in the book of Psalms David prays to God using the phrase, "deliver me". It sounds like the first reaction David would have had in Job's situation would have been to cry out to God for deliverance. David never blamed God as the source of his troubles. David was absolutely certain that God was his Deliverer, not his persecutor.

In drastic contrast we see many verses throughout the book of Job in which Job blames God for his troubles. *"For the ar-*

rows of the Almighty are within me; my spirit drinks in their poison; the terrors of God are arrayed against me" (Job 6:4). "*Your hands have made me and fashioned me, an intricate unity; yet You would destroy me*" (Job 10:8). "*He has also kindled His wrath against me, and He counts me as one of His enemies*" (Job 19:11). "*Why do you persecute me as God does, and are not satisfied with my flesh?*" (Job 19:22). Without any doubt, Job does not see God as his deliverer, but rather the source of his troubles.

The more we know our God; the more we know our enemies.

You may have never noticed, but there is an unusual pattern in many of David's Psalms which can give us insight into an additional benefit of having a close personal relationship with God. Often before, during, or after praising God, David directly references the destruction of his enemies. In fact, the words "enemy" and "enemies" are mentioned 106 times in the book of Psalms. Both of the previous references to David's psalms spoke of God delivering David from his enemies, while in a previous reference we saw Job referring to himself as God's enemy (Job 19:11). I cannot overstate the significance of the contrast between David and Job's understanding of God!

The more we know our God; the more we know our enemies. The more we realize how much God loves us, the more clearly we are able to discern that we have those who hate us. With this new understanding, do we believe Job had a close relationship with God? Compared to other men of faith Job, in the beginning of his story, seems to be deceived about God's character. For instance, David's friend Jonathan, one of King Saul's sons, was able to rout an enemy army with only his armor bearer's help. This was because Jonathan knew his God and therefore, he understood how to fight against his enemies (1 Samuel 14). Another example is Jehoshaphat. He was able to defeat his enemies by placing worshippers in front of the army because he knew his God and therefore, he understood how to fight his enemies (2 Chronicles 20:20-21). You will find this pattern is consistent throughout scripture, and it can be very revealing about someone's relationship with God.

Job is completely unaware of any source other than God to blame for his troubles. *"The earth is given into the hand of the wicked. He covers the faces of its judges. <u>If it is not He, who else can it be</u>?"* (Job 9:24). Job admits here that He is clueless about his enemies. David, as a young shepherd, had spent so much time alone with the Lord that, even at a young age, he had been courageously inspired to kill the formidable enemies of his sheep: the lion and the bear. In stark contrast, there is no will to fight in Job. All we see is his unbelievable resolve to bear up under an attack. I believe this misunderstood resolve is the very reason that the story of Job is the longest book in the Bible about one individual. Job was one incredibly resolute individual. However, once he meets God personally, the story ends rather quickly. This proves Job's need for a heart change which was God's intention all along. This was the end intended by the Lord spoken of in James 5:11.

CHAPTER 4

IS IT GOD'S FAULT?

Why do we blame God?

A tendency of our sin nature is to shift responsibility by blaming someone else. This makes us susceptible to Satan's temptation to blame God. Hopefully this book will make you aware of this weakness, so that it will no longer take you by surprise. Job did not know who to blame, but what logic is there for any of us to blame God? If we do not know who to blame, at the very least it makes more sense to blame an enemy. Our Creator, and loving heavenly Father, should be the last suspect on our list, not the first.

Wouldn't an insurance policy that blamed the damage from a tornado as "an act of Satan" be closer to the truth than one which said "an act of God"? Does God maliciously kill people whom He created for a purpose? *"For we are His workmanship, created in Christ Jesus for good works, which God prepared beforehand that we should walk in them"* (Ephesians 2:10). If Satan is not the direct cause of a catastrophe, couldn't the cause be traced to the original sin which entered the earth by His temptation? Would this not, in the very least, make Satan an accessory? The least likely scenario would be that God destroyed His own creation. People are the objects of God's affection. God esteemed man to be worth the life of His only Son. What sense would it make for Him to destroy the very ones upon whom He Himself has placed such a high value? The reason this is so ridiculous is because it is a lie from Hell sent to undermine our understanding of God.

The Bible is very clear about the far reaching effects of sin, yet many times we are more comfortable blaming God instead.

Much of the time the responsibility for the tragedies we face in this life falls on mankind's original choice to misuse the authority God gave him by freely choosing to rebel. The repercussions of man's original sin can still be seen in all of creation. *"Because the creation itself also will be delivered from the bondage of corruption into the glorious liberty of the children of God. <u>For we know that the whole creation groans and labors</u> with birth pangs together until now"* (Romans 8:21-22). The Bible is very clear about the far reaching effects of sin, yet many times we are more comfortable blaming God instead. Part of our focus on blaming others (including God) is that it allows us to be more comfortable with the repercussions of our own rebellion.

Most of the time we have some part to play in the events of our lives. I am not saying we are responsible when something randomly out of our control happens to us. I am saying that blaming God causes us not to ask the harder question: "Is part of this my fault?" or when our answer to that question is no, then: "Who is trying to destroy me?" It would be better to rest in the knowledge that we do not understand, rather than to blame God Who could never be guilty. Most of the time it is simply too easy for us to blame any unexplainable event on God.

What are the limitations of a sovereign God?

The above question seems rather contradictory, but it is not. As we saw earlier a sovereign is one who possesses supreme power or one who exercises supreme authority. This definition is used to refer to the authority of a king who is called a sovereign.

Is it God's Fault?

The problem with understanding sovereignty is that most people equate absolute authority with absolute control and these are two separate things. Any government, even a democracy, has the authority to enforce the rule of law on its citizens, but if those citizens are prepared to pay the consequences, they have the free will to rebel against that authority. In any governed group of people, events take place that are outside of the will of those in authority. <u>Authority has never meant absolute control over the will of those under authority</u>. Prisons are full of prisoners who chose to exercise their free will over the authority of the law of the land. Both they and their victims are paying a heavy price for their selfish acts of rebellion.

The real problem with understanding sovereignty lies in our failure to comprehend why God would place such a high value on our free will. God is not controlling. The very nature of love is to believe the best about the one loved and hope he will do the right thing. 1 Corinthians 13:7 says that love believes all things and hopes all things. This is the very nature of God. In any relationship where you see one party controlling the actions of the other party, that relationship is not based on God's kind of love.

The authority of the Holy Spirit only goes as far as our free will.

If we are Christians then we received God's Holy Spirit into our hearts when we accepted Jesus Christ as our Savior. But, even with God living on the inside of us, we still have the free will to choose to disobey the voice of the indwelling Holy Spirit. The authority of the Holy Spirit only goes as far as our free will. We could murder someone while, at the same time, the Holy Spirit is screaming at our conscience to stop. God has placed a very high value on our personal authority, yet most of us would feel more comfortable if God was more controlling. <u>We misunderstand</u>

<u>"sovereignty" as meaning "absolute control" for the very reason that we are more controlling than God</u>. God is not controlling the events on earth; He is in authority over them. The real problems lie with those to whom He delegated authority.

What is delegated authority?

We have already seen that at creation God chose mankind to be His delegated authority on the earth. *"Then God blessed them, and God said to them, 'Be fruitful, and multiply; fill the earth, and subdue it; have dominion over the fish of the sea, over the birds of the air, and over every living thing that moves on the earth'"* (Genesis 1:28). The word <u>delegate</u> means a person who is chosen or elected to vote or act for others. Thus, mankind is to act for God or carry out God's will for Him on the earth. The concept of delegated authority is present in almost all of mankind's organizational structures.

With delegated authority comes the inherent risk involved with trusting someone else.

We are very familiar with delegated authority in the business world. If a Chief Executive Officer (CEO) of a corporation appoints someone to be Chief Financial Officer (CFO), it is understood that the newly appointed CFO is responsible for all the corporation's financial operations. It is also understood that he is to represent the CEO's personal regard for ethics in his delegated position of authority over the financials. The CFO will spend some time determining how meticulous his financial reports need to be. This determination will be based on the requirements necessary to fulfill the will of the CEO who is the direct authority over him. At any time however, the CFO could alter the financial data due to the access allowed in his high position of delegated authority. The effect of this could destroy the company and the lives of those who work for it. This outcome would not have been the will of the CEO but only the natural danger involved with delegating authority.

With delegated authority comes the inherent risk involved with trusting someone else. Anyone we trust can let us down in a big way. God's delegation of authority to mankind over all the earth was a very high risk demonstration of His trust. Mankind failed God's trust by listening to the lies of the serpent rather than following the known will of the Authority over him. Man chose to exercise his free will to pick another option and, as they say, the rest is history.

Why does God delegate authority?

Since God is omniscient (all knowing) and omnipotent (all powerful) why doesn't He just control everything? God could obviously do a better job than we have in managing the affairs of earth. So, why doesn't He just take over? The real underlining question is this: Why did God give us free will knowing we would make such a mess of things? The answer is very simple: **God's highest priority is relationship!**

God is willing to put up with the effects of rebellion in order to maintain genuine relationship with us.

To have a genuine relationship with someone, the relationship must not be manipulated and/or controlled in any way. Both parties involved must have the autonomy to choose to leave the relationship at any time. If God were to take away our freedom of choice, He would lose the possibility of genuine relationship with mankind and God's highest priority is that relationship. The proof that this is true is the level of risk God is willing to take in order to keep that relationship. There are an unfathomable number of actions taking place every day that are opposed to God's will. However, for God to remove the individual authority of free will would also remove our ability to freely choose a relationship with Him. And, God is willing to put up with the effects of rebellion in order to maintain genuine relationship with us.

How does false sovereignty clash in the real world?

Satan's distorted version of sovereignty is a loaded trap which is easily sprung by the circumstances of this fallen world. Satan's lie of false sovereignty says God is in **control** of everything that happens, but this is totally different from His having **authority** over everything that happens. If a person buys into this lie, then his natural desire for things to go well will quickly proceed to an internal anger at the controlling God who is the One ultimately responsible for disturbing his peace and rest. **One's belief in an all-controlling God will ultimately mean God will receive all of the blame for the difficulties in their life.** This internal anger will grow with any increase in trauma, reaching a point where reverencing God would be so hypocritical that it will no longer be worth it. Job reaches this point in Job 6:14, *"To him who is afflicted, kindness should be shown by his friend, <u>even though he forsakes the fear of the Almighty</u>."*

Let me be perfectly clear: God loves you. If something bad happens to you, it does not come from God. Many of you may have grown up in church singing a little children's song that went like this: "Jesus loves me this I know for the Bible tells me so." As we get older many of us begin to question the truthfulness of that song. The root cause of this questioning is found again in our desire to make sense of our world. **The chaos in our world**

comes from sin; not from God. *"For God is not the author of confusion but of peace"* (1 Corinthians 14:33a).

The Bible explains the importance of being like a child. *"Then Jesus called a little child to Him, set him in the midst of them, and said, 'Assuredly, I say to you, unless you are converted and become as little children, you will by no means enter the kingdom of heaven. Therefore whoever humbles himself as this little child is the greatest in the kingdom of heaven'"* (Matthew 18:2-4). As adults, we would rather have the wrong answer in order to feel justified in our anger than simply trust God. As we get older, our self-perceived increased knowledge often causes pride when the child-like humility of believing in God's goodness is all we need. <u>God is our rewarder, not our destroyer</u>. (Hebrews 11:6).

The redefining of sovereignty is a strategic Satanic deception to get us to blame God for our trouble.

Here is a fact that we must all face. In this fallen world, which we were born into, bad things happen; things outside of the will of a good God. We can decide to blame God for the bad, which would be a mistake because God is love. Or, we can choose to blame our mutual enemy, the devil, who is responsible, either directly or indirectly, through his temptation of man. Let me be very clear: the redefining of sovereignty is a strategic Satanic deception to get us to blame God for our trouble. This strategy has proven to be very effective in distancing people from the love of God. According to 2 Corinthians 10:3-5 anything that is coming against our relationship with God is from our enemy, Satan. His singular target is to corrupt our knowledge of what God is really like. Satan is terrified that if we ever know how good God really is, we will trust and obey Him in every area of our lives.

The early church was comprised of a group of people who believed that God loved them and were willing to lay down their own lives to take that love to the world. No matter how outmatched the fight appears to be, Satan will lose every time to anyone who truly knows the love of God. A perfect example of this truth would be David who, as a youth, defeated the giant Goliath. Satan must attack the knowledge of God's true character because people who know the love of God and possess that same love are extremely dangerous to his agenda. Satan's perversion of sovereignty is his flanking maneuver against the goodness of God. This tactic does not directly say God is bad, therefore it has proven to be even more dangerous than a frontal assault on God's character.

Does someone have to be guilty?

The tragic death of a minister's teenage daughter happened several years ago. She was a youth minister who traveled extensively speaking at youth conferences. She loved the Lord with all of her heart and was a great role model for other young adults. While traveling to a conference she was killed in a plane crash. As devastating as the death of his daughter was, this father would not stop pursuing God for answers. This was because he knew God was good and the accident could not have been God's fault. After earnestly seeking for an answer the Lord appeared to this father in a dream and showed him the reason his daughter had died. A mechanic who was required to perform a critically needed maintenance procedure had done it incorrectly. Basically, this mechanic chose to take a short cut instead of the required maintenance. This short cut had resulted in his daughter's death. Before sin entered the world, this procedure would have been done correctly. After sin's introduction, this man's freewill was tempted and he chose laziness rather than the necessary diligence.

We are in the middle of a war zone where bad things happen all the time.

We want justice; we want answers. If we really want the truth of who is responsible then we have to start with the premise that God did not do something evil. <u>We must eliminate the option that it was God's fault</u>. We live in a fallen world where man's freewill to choose sin can often effect the outcome of our lives. We are in the middle of a war zone where bad things happen all the time. How we deal with these events demonstrates how clearly we understand the world in which we live and God Who loves us. Often we cannot pin the blame for our trouble on one source. It is the cumulative effect of sin.

What undermines our relationship with God the most?

I love the analogy of the two horses pulling against each other. One represents faith, while the other horse represents unbelief. In this analogy it is not only how much faith you have, but how much unbelief is pulling in the opposite direction. The horse of faith, without unbelief pulling against it, could accomplish anything. I think this analogy represents accurately what is going on in our hearts. But, which horse will win? The obvious answer is the strongest horse. And, what makes the horse strong is what you feed it. Time with God and fellow believers will feed the horse of faith, but what is the primary food source for our unbelief?

I believe that the daily cares and concerns of this world (Matthew 13:3-9,18-23) are the fundamental food source for the horse of unbelief. The problems we face every day draw our attention away from the eternal perspective of who we are. I believe Job, with all of his wealth and servants and responsibilities, had been pulled into a place of unbelief. When we focus on our physical needs we feed our horse of unbelief. We must make a conscious effort to focus on who we are in Christ and our eternal future without getting bogged down in the affairs of this life. *"You therefore <u>must endure hardship</u> as a good soldier of Jesus Christ. No one <u>engaged in warfare entangles himself with the affairs of this life</u>, that he may please him who enlisted him as a soldier"* (2 Timothy 2:3-4).

How well we overcome the difficulties in this life will depend on how well we maintain an eternal perspective.

Everything in this life will not go the way we want; we must endure hardship. We are no longer in the Garden of Eden. How well we overcome the difficulties in this life will depend on how well we maintain an eternal perspective. If we focus on the problem, we are feeding our horse of unbelief and this will destroy our faith in God. I have never met a negative person who has great faith. Never! Such persons became negative by focusing on the problem, and focusing on the problem destroyed their faith.

The opportunity for the cares and concerns of this world to steal our eternal destiny is a theme repeated throughout the Bible. Ruth chose to follow her mother-in-law, Naomi, even with little hope for a future while her sister-in-law, Orpah, chose the easier route to meet her physical needs (Ruth 1:8-16). We never hear of Orpah again. In contrast, Ruth is placed in the lineage of Christ Himself (Ruth 4:13-17). Esau was so focused on his hunger that he sold his inheritance as a firstborn son. Where would Esau be if he had decided to wait thirty minutes to eat because he honored his birthright which came from God more than the temporary satisfaction of food? Esau would have been the one to carry on his father's spiritual heritage if he had maintained an eternal perspective. (Genesis 25:29-34).

Most of us do not want to have unbelief, but our focus can often be on our daily difficulties which starve our faith and feed our unbelief. Jesus spoke of this in the Parable of the Sower; *"Now he who received seed among the thorns is he who hears the word, and <u>the cares of this world and the deceitfulness of riches</u> choke the word, and he becomes unfruitful"* (Matthew 13:22). Job is an example to me of someone who was so bogged down in this life that he was unable to perceive what was going on spiritually. These daily distractions could also explain why Job was unaware that he had an enemy.

How fast can our desire for rest be tested?

Our relationship with God is not really tested until things do not go the way we planned. Our reaction to events that are opposite from what we would have desired is an indication of how much our life is being driven by the same desire for rest that we see in Job. What makes us angry and, how quickly do we get angry? For most of us this is not a comfortable subject. Many of us know we should not become angry so quickly, but we are embarrassed because we do. What is really happening when we become angry so quickly? Most of the time it is because we were inconvenienced or disrespected in some way. If we get angry in traffic it is usually because someone made a decision that cost us time or they were disrespectful of our rights on the road. It can be easy for us to become angry in relationships because we can become offended when we feel like we have been taken for granted by someone close to us.

CAN I TRUST GOD

Someone who quickly becomes angry has become self-focused, being driven by their internal desire for ease and rest.

Our unspoken desires for everything to go well can quickly turn unexpected bad news or unplanned inconvenience into a flashpoint of anger that can often surprise us. Remember, we were made for a perfect world, so this desire is not at all unnatural. It is, however, totally irrational because we no longer live in the Garden of Eden. We live in a world of chaos caused by the effects of sin. Someone who quickly becomes angry has become self-focused, being driven by their internal desire for ease and rest. Focusing on ease and rest often leads to self-centeredness. People with "anger issues" can even vent their selfish desire onto others when things don't go well. We have all been around people with whom we have been reluctant to share bad news because we feared their reaction.

Bad things happen which are outside of our control. Often things do not go as planned. If we anticipate this as the reality of the world we live in, our reactions to adverse circumstances can be kept to a reasonable level of frustration. Anything above this is usually an indication that we have bought into the same false understanding of ease and rest that Job had. Now, to Job's credit, he did not get angry quickly, but this is only because he had been expecting bad things to happen. *"For the thing I greatly feared has come upon me, and what I dreaded has happened to me"* (Job 3:25). Although this is a more realistic approach to his environment, the problem lies in his belief that God would be the source of the catastrophes which would be coming. That is why it takes so long for God to get through to Job because Job is blaming the wrong source for his trouble.

Is it God's Fault?

If we believe God loves us and is only looking out for our best interest, there is no longer a reason to dread what He might do.

A majority of Christians will never grow beyond an apparent ceiling in their relationship with God because of the same misunderstanding which Job had. <u>Bad things that have happened or that are going to happen in the future are not God's plan for our lives; neither are they God's fault, and they are definitely not God's will.</u> Most of the time it is due to living in a world in rebellion outside of God's perfect plan that is causing your adverse circumstances. We live in a world which is full of people influenced by a lying devil who is deceiving us toward evil. This is the nature of Satan's recruiting process. He must tempt someone to believe a lie in order to get that person's agreement to do his will.

Once we understand the reality of this spiritual war, we are able to move forward in our relationship with God because the barrier of distrust has been removed. If we believe God loves us and is only looking out for our best interest, there is no longer a reason to dread what He might do. There will also arise a desire to fight against an enemy who is deceiving so many toward evil. There was a will to fight in David against his enemy because he knew the true heart of God, but there was no will to fight in Job because he did not accurately know God's heart.

How does Satan use the book of Job most effectively?

The most effective strategy to defeat the purposes of God would be to persuade His followers that it is pointless to fight.

What would be the most effective strategy to defeat the purposes of God? Would it be to kill every Christian? When Satan has deceived the hearts of men to kill Christians the church has flourished. It is even said that the church has been built on the blood of martyrs. The most effective strategy to defeat the purposes of God would be to persuade His followers that it is pointless to fight. To this end, Satan has hijacked the book of Job to promote the misunderstanding of sovereignty. If God can be blamed for evil as well as good, it is pointless to resist His will by fighting against Him. After all, who could win a fight against God?

Although I do not admire the devil in any way, I can, however, appreciate the brilliance of his evil strategy. Consider the story of David and Goliath. If someone knows God is on his side, he is inspired to fight against his enemies. In fact, the more we know that God is for us the more we are aware of who is against us. Through this highly effective deception, Satan has blinded Job's eyes to the love of God. Job is confused. He doesn't know if God is his Deliverer or his adversary. Job chooses not to fight back because he believes his tragedy is from God and who could successfully oppose the will of God? This may be the craftiest of Satan's deceptions and, sadly, it permeates the body of Christ today.

We cannot be on the offensive if we believe God is the problem.

God loves us and will never ever be against us. I believe God wants to use this book to establish His love more firmly in our hearts. The lie that God will harm us is satanic. As we embrace the truth of God's unconditional love, we will not only resist this lie, but will find our place in the fight against the enemies of God. Jesus said, *"...and on this rock I will build My church and the gates of Hades shall not prevail against it"* (Matthew 16:18b). Notice that the church is on the offensive and hell is on the defensive. We cannot be on the offensive if we believe God is the problem.

Many people have misinterpreted the above verse to mean that the church will be able to withstand hell which is attacking her. The problem with that interpretation is that gates are a defense against attack. In Judges 16:3 Samson removed the doors and bars of an enemy's city gate and put them on a nearby hill. Because he had proven the city was defenseless against the power God had given him, his enemies soon began trying to find the source of his strength to destroy it. Jesus clearly was saying that the defenses of hell would not be able to withstand the attack of the church. Specifically, He was referring to those who had the revelation of the understanding of Christ as the Son of God.

The misunderstanding that we are in a defensive posture can stop us from laying hands on the sick. It can stop us from casting out a demon. It can stop us from going forward when our finances are not there. It can make us abandon the call of God on our lives when circumstances are difficult. It is easy to believe the lie: "If I am following God, then He <u>should</u> make my life easy." **We must understand that we are at war and there will be resistance!** We have to establish in our hearts that, even though we face opposition, we are certain of one undeniable fact: that opposition is not from God! If the Apostle Paul had thought for one moment that God was causing the opposition against him, he could not have endured the malicious persecution coming against him. We must all make a conscious decision to follow God no matter the obstacles. This decision will be much easier to make when we are certain God is not causing the obstacles.

CHAPTER 5

HOW DOES GOD DEAL WITH OUR DECEIVED HEARTS?

How does God guide us when our understanding is the biggest obstacle?

Once we accept Jesus as our Lord, God sends His Holy Spirit to live in our hearts. *"And because you are sons, God has sent forth the Spirit of His Son into your hearts, crying out, 'Abba, Father!'"* (Galatians 4:6). The Holy Spirit will guide us to the truth because He is the Spirit of Truth. *"However, when He, the Spirit of truth, has come, He will guide you into all truth; for He will not speak on His own authority, but whatever He hears He will speak; and He will tell you things to come"* (John 16:13). <u>Although the Holy Spirit is all-powerful, He limits His authority in our lives to the agreement of our free will.</u>

Many believers would rather hold onto their perceived right to blame God , than relinquish this stronghold!

The Holy Spirit will not force us to accept the truth. Satan's deceptions are always available as an alternate choice just as they were in the Garden of Eden. By an act of our free will, we must choose to listen to the voice of God's indwelling Spirit. God must deal with the obstacle of our deceived heart by having us freely choose to renounce our stronghold of blaming someone for our troubles. This desire is birthed from our need for relief from the difficulties we face in this fallen world. This stronghold can be so powerful that we often allow it to override the voice of God's Holy Spirit in us. Our desire for relief can lead us to blame our heavenly Father Who loves us the most. Frankly, many believers would rather hold onto their perceived right to blame God than relinquish this stronghold!

God's plan for our future is the plan that will bring the most fulfillment in our lives. *"For I know the thoughts that I think toward you, says the Lord, thoughts of peace and not of evil, <u>to give you a future</u> and a hope"* (Jeremiah 29:11). As any good parent, your heavenly Father desires you to have the most abundant life possible. *"...I have come that they may have life, and that they may have it more abundantly"* (John 10:10b). But, what is God supposed to do when the biggest obstacle to our abundant life is our own deceived heart? God loves us, but how does He relate to us when we don't know that He does? <u>Our unbelief in God's love for us is the most common relational problem that He must deal with</u>. God chose His best servant Job as the perfect example of this relational problem.

If you are going to have a strong spiritual life, it must be built on the strongest foundation which is: God loves me. *"For no other foundation can anyone lay than that which is laid, which is Jesus Christ"* (1 Corinthians 3:11). God sending His Son to die on our behalf is the undeniable confirmation of His love for us. Without the foundation of knowing God's love, any unexpected event can turn our lives into chaos. Unlike Job, we live after the irrefutable evidence of God's love. *"For God so loved the world that He gave His only begotten Son, that whoever believes in Him should not perish but have everlasting life"* (John 3:16). Any foundational understanding of God which deviates from "God loves me" is based upon lies from Satan sent to steal our abundant life.

Job has one big problem: he does not understand that God loves him.

How Does God Deal with Our Deceived Hearts?

We can be absolutely certain of one undeniable truth in the story of Job: **God loves Job**. To approach Job's story from any other perspective is to approach it with a deceived heart which will result in an incorrect interpretation. Having my feet planted on the ground is analogous to being firmly grounded in the understanding of God's love for me. Standing in a rocking chair is analogous to being grounded in something other than the love of God for me. On a foundation other than God's love, almost anything can "rock" your world. Job has one big problem: he does not understand that God loves him. When tragedy strikes, the weak foundation of resting on his own performance results in vulnerability during this attack from the devil.

God has a plan for Job's life and this fact is mentioned in James 5:11, *"Indeed we count them blessed who endure. You have heard of the perseverance of Job, <u>and seen the end intended by the Lord</u> - that the Lord is very compassionate and merciful."* When we approach the story of Job the events can often seem random in nature, but this is not what the word of God says. The word <u>end</u> means to set out for a definite point or goal; properly, the point aimed at as a limit. I am not insinuating that God caused the tragedy in Job's life, the Bible says Satan did, but God did have a definite plan for Job's eternal destiny. God's goal for each of us is an abundant life, but without the knowledge of God's love we will never reach that goal.

What do we do when bad things happen?

It is easy to control our demand for answers and our yearning to blame others when things are going well, but the deceptions in our heart manifest quickly when bad things happen. The real test is this: will we believe it's God's fault when things do not go well? We will only know we are completely free from deceptions about God's character if, when tragedy strikes, we fail to consider the possibility of blaming God. For some of us just a flat tire can cause us to point the finger at God. **When are we going to wake up from our deceptions and realize that this world is not perfect anymore? There are nails in the road!** Satan's deception of the concept of sovereignty has caused many people to see only one source to blame: God. Wasn't Satan the one who tempted mankind to sin? Was it not his temptation that resulted in the world falling into chaos? Blaming God seems like an obvious deflection of the spotlight off the guilty party, Satan.

Rather than blaming God, there are some people who internalize the responsibility for the events that take place in their lives. They will even feel guilty for being abused, thinking that it was their fault. This is a devious perversion of the facts as Satan attempts to use shame against us as a weapon. It is important to reject the condemnation of guilt that Satan tries to put on us. If he can get us to believe it is all our fault, then we will feel unworthy of God's love. Our anger, which should be directed outward toward our enemy, will be directed inward toward ourselves. The end result will be the same: a separation from the knowledge of how much God loves us. It is important to realize how God sees us, *"Just as He chose us in Him before the foundation of the world, that we should be <u>holy and without blame</u> before Him in love"* (Ephesians 1:4). If you are having difficulty with feelings of condemnation, please re-read A Word from the Author in the front of this book. God will never condemn you!

The only possible explanation for someone being upset with great news is a twisted understanding of truth.

When I boldly proclaim that bad things are not God's fault, this good news can actually offend some people. If someone has blamed God for a past event, then I just let their guilty party go

How Does God Deal with Our Deceived Hearts?

free. We may be harboring unforgiveness toward God and not even realize it. Why would anyone be upset to discover that their heavenly Father is kinder than they originally thought? The only possible explanation for someone being upset with great news is a twisted understanding of the truth.

If we become agitated or angry when we hear truth, there is a distinct possibility that we are blaming God for some past experience. Keeping the option of blaming God is one of the main reasons people defend their false understanding of sovereignty rather than accepting the truth. We all desire easy answers because we yearn for comfort and rest, but instead trouble comes. On this earth we all have exactly the same problem that Job had; *"I am not at ease, nor am I quiet; I have no rest, for trouble comes"* (Job 3:26). The real question is: how will we deal with it? Will we choose <u>not</u> to blame God?

If Job could not blame God, he was not sure who was at fault.

If someone believes God is the guilty party, and that belief is exposed as false, they no longer have any explanation for what happened. This is the <u>exact</u> same problem that Job was facing. If Job could not blame God, he was not sure who was at fault. Remember Job 9:24b, *"If it is not He, who else could it be?"* God loves us, so He must lead us into the truth. This means, when faced with the truth, <u>we</u> have to choose to give up our deceptions. **There is a tendency in all of us to want to hold onto our familiar beliefs no matter how misguided.** This is the deceitfulness of the human heart which is spoken of in Jeremiah 17:9. In our hearts we are accustomed to following well-worn deceitful paths. Resisting these familiar paths to blaze a new trail to find the truth is the only course which will lead to our freedom.

CAN I TRUST GOD

Why are we double-minded?

God is either good or He is not, He cannot be both!

What earthly father could be accused of the things that God has been accused of doing to His children? *"If you then, being evil, know how to give good gifts to your children, how much more will your Father who is in heaven give good things to those who ask Him!"* (Matthew 7:11). Did God kill your spouse? Did God take your child? God is either good or He is not, He cannot be both! If God could be both, then He would be in violation of Jesus's teachings on the kingdom, *"But He, knowing their thoughts, said to them: 'Every kingdom divided against itself is brought to desolation, and a house divided against a house falls'"* (Luke 11:17).

The real issue in question is not God's character, it is our double-mindedness. *"If any of you lacks wisdom, let him ask of God, who gives to all liberally and without reproach, and it will be given to him. But let him ask in faith, with no doubting, for he who doubts is like a wave of the sea driven and tossed by the wind. For let not that man suppose that he will receive anything from the Lord; <u>he is a double-minded man, unstable in all his ways</u>"* (James 1:5-8). This verse talks about a double minded man who asks God for wisdom, but doesn't believe that God will give it to him. In the very same way many of us claim that God is good, but secretly believe that He will do us harm.

The Holy Spirit is always bearing witness that God is good, but we are arguing with the Spirit of Truth and choosing to believe God is not "that" good. David's relationship with God is one we would do well to emulate. David knew God's goodness to the core of his being. Remember his words from Psalms 56:9b, *"This I know because **God is for me**."* David was not double-minded on his knowledge of God's love for him. He was sure! Like David, this assurance is what we need to carry out God's will, especially in difficult circumstances.

Has God run out of options with Job?

I want to present the possibility that God has run out of options in His relationship with Job. One thing we are absolutely sure of in God's relationship with Job is this: God loves Job. How has God been demonstrating His love to Job? He has been blessing Job with both children and material possessions. *"And seven sons and three daughters were born to him. Also, his possessions were seven thousand sheep, three thousand camels, five hundred yoke of oxen, five hundred female donkeys, and a very large household, so that this man was the greatest of all the people of the East"* (Job 1:2-3). God's heart is to bless His children, but what if His blessing is not helping with the most important part of our lives which is our relationship with Him? How is God going to convince Job of His love? Will 1,000 more sheep communicate His love? Will more children express God's love enough for Job to notice? Saying Job is the greatest man in the east is the same as saying he is the richest man in Asia. The point is, Job is wealthy and the blessings are not working to strengthen his relationship with God. Remember, in all of his tragedy, Job never asks God for help. He is completely clueless as to how much God loves him.

The reason I said God might have run out of options is because He is unable to solve Job's deception through His normal actions of blessing. This is the same relational difficulty God has with most of us and yet, we live after the ultimate blessing of Christ's redemption. What more is God supposed to do to prove His love to us? Should He crucify Jesus again? Somehow, I don't think that will make a difference. What is God supposed to do when His love for us is not being understood?

Why must God take us through our fears?

What we fear is what we respect and honor the most. <u>We have given control of our lives to what we fear.</u> We are instructed many times to fear and reverence God. All other fears must be dethroned because they act as false gods in our lives, they manipulate our thoughts and emotions. The most direct way to conquer the stronghold of any fear is to face that fear. This strips the fear of the control that we have given it over us. Job fears a lack of ease and rest, so as He goes through that fear its power is broken in his life.

<u>With an understanding of God's love, fear would have never dominated Job's life</u> because the knowledge of God's love removes fear. *"There is no fear in love; but perfect love casts out fear, because fear involves torment. But he who fears has not been made perfect in love"* (1 John 4:18). God had the Hebrews face their fear of the Egyptian army so that He could demonstrate to them that His power was much greater than their fear. For years the Egyptians had drowned the unwanted Hebrew children. God showed Himself greater than the fear of drowning in the lives of the Hebrews by having them go through the Red Sea and not around it. The Egyptian army suffered the same fate as the many Hebrew infants they had drowned in the Nile River.

Fear has a controlling power to distort our perspective of the truth. Job was rich in family, in lands, and in livestock. In fact, His life was blessed and prosperous in every way. But, how did Job live his life? *"For the thing I <u>greatly feared</u> has come upon me, and what I <u>dreaded</u> has happened to me"* (Job 3:25). This extremely blessed man was living his life in excessive anxiety of what could happen to him. His decision to give into these fears had stripped him of the enjoyment of his life. These fears had so dominated Job's life that they had distorted his view of God.

Do our fears have the power to change our future?

Job has no evidence to support the possibility that God will one day do him harm, yet he lives in the dread of it. Job's fear is rooted in his misunderstanding of God. He thinks God is good and bad; that He can bless him as well as harm him. Job lives completely in the good, yet imagines in dread the arrival of the bad. He is certain that the bad is coming. He doesn't know when, but it could be any minute and he is sure it will be dreadful. Isn't this an exact picture of what actually happened? Did Job help to manifest his own future by dwelling upon it? *"For as he* thinks *in his heart, so is he."* (Proverbs 23:7a). The word thinks here means gatekeeper. Job left the gate of his mind open. He had not taken captive the thoughts that were lies about God (2 Corinthians 10:5), but had welcomed them into his heart. Therefore, these uncaptured thoughts were built into a stronghold of deception which all of God's loving efforts had been unable to penetrate.

There is an attribute of love found in 1 Corinthians 13:4 which says that love does not parade itself. The word for parade in the King James Version of the Bible is vaunteth which means to brag. This attribute of love is also an attribute of God. God does not appear to us and brag about His great love. He presents the truth of His love and allows us to choose the truth over the lies we hear about Him. In this God seems to be extreme, even to the point of manifesting to us as we imagine Him to be. David was aware of this about God. *"With the merciful You show Yourself merciful; with the blameless man You show Yourself blameless;*

with the pure You show Yourself pure; and <u>with the devious You show Yourself shrewd</u>" (Psalm 18:25-26).

The way God chooses to reveal Himself to Job is interesting. He shows up proclaiming His works (Job 38-40). The reason God does this is because Job has decided to judge himself based on his own performance. God follows Job's lead by speaking of a few things He has accomplished. This strategy exposes the deception in Job's heart. Job believed God's love for him was based on his performance. God is making it very clear, through the humbling of Job, that His acceptance of us is not based on our performance.

God's approach is very strong evidence of how far Job had strayed from God's intended path of unconditional love and acceptance. God's blessing was intended to convey His love to Job. However, in Job's mind, his blessings were the result of his performance. Job believes he has done everything right, so how could God cause it to go so wrong? Job's attitude is: "I guess God is wrong, because I know I'm right!" This is definitely not the smartest choice of the available options. Here is some advice which will save all of us from many painful chapters in our own lives. If the choice is between us or God being wrong, we should just pick ourselves every time.

God must show Himself to us as we see Him so that He will be recognized. Only then is He able to transform our thinking into what He is really like.

When God physically appears to Job, He appears in a whirlwind, one of the most fearful things on earth. *"Then the Lord answered Job out of the whirlwind, and said:"* (Job 38:1). God manifested the way Job had pictured in his heart. To the fearful Job, God showed Himself terrifying. God did not do this because it was what He wanted, but what Job wanted. God must show Himself to us as we see Him so that He will be recognized. Only then is He able to transform our thinking to reveal what He is really like.

God did this with Elijah in 1 Kings 19:11-13. God passed by and there was wind, earthquake, and fire, but He was not in them; He was in the still small voice. God led Elijah from his current understanding of Him as a displayer of supernatural acts to a God who desired personal relationship. God does the same thing with Job; it only takes longer because Job's heart is so deceived about God's true character.

This same principle is also seen in the Parable of the Talents (Matthew 25:14-30). In verse 24 the lazy servant says, he <u>knew</u> the landowner to be a hard man. The landowner, who represents God, doesn't deny the servant's beliefs, but uses the servant's own understanding to assess judgment. *"...you <u>knew</u> that I reap where I have not sown, and gather where I have not scattered seed...so take the talent from him..."* (Matthew 25:26b,28a). Notice that the landowner, representing God, does not defend himself. Somehow God judges our actions based on our limited understanding of Him, but this is not where He wants us to stop in His relationship with us. God wants us to see Him in the truth of Who He really is.

What does God's commendation of Job reveal about their relationship?

Twice God addresses Satan with this repeated commendation of Job, *"...Have you considered My servant Job, that there is none like him on the earth, a blameless and upright man, one who fears God and shuns evil?"* (Job 1:8 & Job 2:3). Once again, for the purpose of discernment, let's compare Job's commendation to those of other men of God. Here God is calling Job His servant, but we already know that He called David, "...a man after His/My own Heart" (I Samuel 13:14, Acts 13:22). God refers to Abraham as His friend. (James 2:23). He also refers to Moses as a friend (Exodus 33:11). God desires a relationship with us that is closer than that of Master/servant. *"Therefore you are no longer a slave but a son, and if a son, then an heir of God through Christ"* (Galatians 4:7). *"And it shall be, in that day, says the Lord, that you will call Me 'My Husband', and no longer call Me 'My Master',"* (Hosea 2:16). My point is simply this: though honorable, the designation of servant is not one of God's highest compliments.

If we evaluate our relationship with God on our performance then we will view Job's commendation as the highest of all commendations.

To explain God's assessment of Job, I would like to state two truthful, yet different, commendations of my older son and have you pick which one is the most significant. The first: he is an upright and Godly son who does everything I ask him to do. The second: he exhibits such a heart for God and for me that he makes me want to be a better man. These are both true, but there is no doubt which one is the most significant. The first commendation is based on performance which is a much weaker foundation than the second which is based on relationship. God can be proud of your performance, yet He still understands that you have a long way to go in growing in relationship with Him. This is how God sees Job. His commendation is all about Job's performance, which is stellar, yet he is still nowhere close to God's desire that he be a friend or someone "after His Own heart."

How Does God Deal with Our Deceived Hearts?

When someone wants to ardently defend Job's character, it is an indication that they are on a foundation of works and not a foundation of love.

If we evaluate our relationship with God on our performance then we will view Job's commendation as the highest of all commendations. Job becomes someone we wish to emulate, so that we too will receive a similar commendation. If you are doing this, <u>please stop and realize that you have been deceived</u>. When we want our heavenly Father to praise us based on our performance, we are seeking the wrong commendation. This is not what we should desire! Unconditional love and acceptance is the foundation of the gospel, never our performance. When someone wants to ardently defend Job's character, it is an indication that they are on a foundation of works and not a foundation of love.

God wants us to come to Him based on our identity in Christ, not based on our works.

To say Job has bad character would be a direct contradiction of God Himself. God said that there was no one like Job on the earth, and He also said that he was blameless. I am not saying God is wrong; I am only saying that there is a higher commendation which is not based on performance. <u>A servant's worth is based on performance, while a son's worth is based on his identity</u>. God wants us to come to Him based on our identity in Christ, not based on our works. Job does not know he is accepted apart from his works, but he will. This is *"…the end intended by the Lord…"* spoken of in James 5:11. This is the place God wants to take all of us in our spiritual journey. God wants us to know that His love has no qualifications. Notice: God considered Job blameless even though he was severely deceived. In like manner, God does not hold our ignorance against us (Ephesians 1:4).

It can be easy to get in an argument with someone over the book of Job. It is because their personal value may have been placed on their works in an attempt to earn their heavenly Father's approval. By challenging Job's works foundation, we might be perceived as attacking someone's personal belief system. <u>We are literally undermining their spiritual foundation</u>. They believe God loves them if they are doing, if they are not sinning, if they are upright, if they are blameless. When they read Job's commendation, they believe that is as high as one can get and, for performance-based acceptance, that is true. This is why God picked Job as the example. He is doing everything right; he just doesn't have the most important part — a relationship with God based on His unconditional love.

Being upright and having accurate understanding should never be considered synonymous.

We often judge other religions and denominations based on their understanding. We assume that because they do not have the understanding that we have then they could not have a heart for God. This is a deception caused by our judgmental sin nature. <u>Job is the most upright person on the earth</u>! But, at the same time he has a very incomplete understanding of the true nature of God. Being upright and having accurate understanding should never be considered synonymous. Anyone of us can be extremely sincere and still be sincerely wrong.

I was in a church where the pastor read this commendation of Job with such passion it was incredible to behold. It was loud, forceful, and passionate, but I could never comprehend what he was so excited about. I now understand that He wanted to hear the same commendation from his heavenly Father. Winning an argument with someone with this misunderstanding is impossible. All we can do is demonstrate our personal relationship with

How Does God Deal with Our Deceived Hearts?

God as a living reality. We can show them that there is more to a relationship with God than what we do. **There are many leaders in the body of Christ who are some of the finest people on earth, but just like Job, they do not realize that their Heavenly Father accepts them, regardless of their performance.**

As we enter the end of this age, God is desiring that there be a group of people who know Him in the depth of their hearts. Because of their relationship, these people will not blame God for anything that Satan tries to throw at them. Like John, they will know their position as the one whom Jesus loves and stand in the authority of God's love. They will possess the same heart as David, *"The Lord is on my side; I will not fear. What can man do to me?"* (Psalm 118:6). They will be immune to Satan's deceptions because their foundation is based on the knowledge of God's love. **"This I know, because God is for me"** (Psalm 56:9b). They will not let go of God, regardless of what they see happening around them.

CHAPTER 6

WHAT IS JOB'S MINDSET?

Why is Job not listed in the hall of faith in Hebrews 11?

Although Job is the longest book about one of God's followers, Job is not mentioned in a list of people of faith in Hebrews 11. Why? I think the answer can be found in Hebrews 11:6, *"But without faith it is impossible to please Him, for he who comes to God must believe that He is, and that He is a rewarder of those who diligently seek Him."* The word <u>rewarder</u> means remunerator, which is to pay in like kind. This is saying that when you pursue God, He will pay you back for your pursuit of Him because God is a good God. I think the reason Job is not listed in the hall of faith is because he is unclear about God's goodness.

Authentic faith rests on believing in the goodness of God.

Using Hebrews 11:6 as a requirement for faith, I am unsure if Job had what we might consider New Testament faith. James 2:19 says, *"You believe that there is one God. You do well. Even the demons believe—and tremble!"* With this statement it is clear that literally any being can believe that God exists, but true faith is trusting in the belief of God as a rewarder. Job was a believer who followed God despite what he believed about His character, but authentic faith rests on believing in the goodness of God. We don't have an account of Job's relationship with God before tragedy strikes, but once it does there is little evidence that he ever had any revelation about the goodness of God.

What is commitment doctrine and how do we recognize it?

After Job loses everything He owns in a matter of minutes, including all of his children, he laments and makes one of the most famous statements in all of the Bible. *"The Lord gave, and the Lord has taken away; blessed be the name of the Lord"* (Job 1:21b). Remember, Job later retracts this statement by saying that He did not know what he was talking about (Job 42:3). Since Job's original statement was incorrect, it is vitally important to understand what was wrong with his thinking when He made this statement. It is even more crucial because many people have embraced the above statement as a Biblical truth even though it is later retracted by Job himself. I believe Job had developed what I call a "commitment doctrine", which I will explain and illustrate.

God created us to succeed; we were never intended to experience failure.

A commitment doctrine is when our ability to keep our commitments to God is emphasized more than the free gift of God's love. The reason Job's statement in Job 1:21, can hold so much meaning for some is because there is a tendency in the human spirit to be an overcomer. In the core of who we are, none of us wants to be a quitter. This is because God created us to succeed; we were never intended to experience failure. We all place a very high value on overcoming the obstacles that we face in this life. We admire that trait in anyone, especially in ourselves.

When this trait passed from the perfect world we were created for (with a foundation of unconditional love) to this fallen world (with a foundation of performance), it became perverted. Quitting, to many of us, means we are failures. Our desire to hold onto God, even if we feel He has wronged us, is evidence

What is Job's Mindset?

of a commitment doctrine. Our need to be committed is driven by two things. The first is our false belief that the more we do for God the more we will be accepted by Him. The second is the fear of the shame we would feel if we were to fail.

Job is the pinnacle of a man strengthening himself in his own commitment, and he is highly respected by those who embrace a commitment doctrine.

Job must have been a hard worker. In an agrarian society, it would have been impossible to become rich without hard work coupled with the tenacity to overcome failures. There would have been crop failures, animal diseases, drought, enemy raids, insect infestation, etc.; but Job had overcome them all to become the wealthiest man in that part of the world. Because Job misunderstood the goodness of God's heart, he had mistakenly assumed that at some point God would be one of the obstacles which he would have to overcome. Job resolved to brace himself for the day this would happen. To his credit he executed his plan flawlessly, at least for a while. Job is the pinnacle of a man strengthening himself in his own commitment, and he is highly respected by those who take great pride in their own commitment.

God will never be impressed with any commitment which has <u>our</u> ability to perform as its foundation.

This doctrine is all about our own works and has nothing to do with the free gift of God's love which He gives us despite the strength of our commitment. In our own strength we were all hopeless failures, but God is the one who freely gave us the victory provided by His Son, Jesus. The only way to overcome in this world we find ourselves in is to accept the offer of Jesus's victory on our behalf. *"But thanks be to God, <u>who gives us the victory</u> through our Lord Jesus Christ"* (1 Corinthians 15:57).

Standing in the strength of our own ability to stay committed devalues the work Jesus did to achieve our victory.

God will never be impressed with any commitment which has our ability to perform as its foundation. Job will have to have his mind renewed (Job 42:5), but it takes Him a long time to do so because he is so entrenched in his performance-based commitment. If we observe ourselves with similar motivations all we need to do is repent and ask God to show us how to break those old patterns. **God loves everything about us**, even the tenacity He gave us not to quit. God loves us even when we fail. There is only one way to be free from the high value we have placed on our own <u>performance</u>: repent and believe only in Jesus. *"Then they said to Him, 'What shall we do, that we may work the works of God?' Jesus answered and said to them, '<u>This is the work of God, that you believe in Him whom He sent</u>'"* (John 6:28-29).

What are some examples of commitment doctrine?

A great biblical example of someone overly focused on their commitment was one of Jesus's closest disciples. *"Peter answered and said to Him, 'Even if all are made to stumble because of You, I will never be made to stumble'"* (Matthew 26:33). Even after being corrected by Jesus Himself (verse 34), Peter is still resolute in his level of commitment. *"Peter said to Him, 'Even if I have to die with You, I will not deny You!' And so said all the disciples"* (Matthew 26:35). The disciples' strength in their own commitment had to fall from the elevated pedestal they had put it upon. But, its fall was especially hard for Peter. It appears from the Biblical account that John may have been the only disciple present for the actual crucifixion. If so, I believe this is not a coincidence as John had been more focused on being the one Jesus loved rather than how committed he was to loving Christ.

What is Job's Mindset?

I once attended a series being taught on the Beatitudes (these are the statements of Jesus at the beginning of His Sermon on the Mount [Matthew 5:1-12], which begin with the word <u>blessed</u>). The series was nine lessons (one for each <u>blessed</u> verse), but the speaker did something very unusual at the beginning of every lesson. I was only able to understand the significance of his actions years later. He began each lesson speaking for five to ten minutes on Matthew 5:1, before proceeding to teach the particular Beatitude for that week. *"And seeing the multitudes, He <u>went up</u> on a mountain, and when He was seated His <u>disciples came to Him</u>."*

The fact that Jesus's disciples <u>came up to Him</u> was emphasized each lesson. There is great value in coming to Jesus and spending time with Him, but the emphasis was on the <u>effort</u> His disciples had made to come to Jesus. They, unlike the multitudes who stayed behind, had climbed a mountain to be with Jesus! This speaker's focus was Jesus's willingness to teach the ones who put forth the <u>effort</u> to come up to Him. Every week the speaker emphasized the <u>work</u> of the disciples to come to Jesus. He stressed that the disciples had put more <u>effort</u> in coming to Jesus than His other followers. This minister placed more emphasis on the commitment of the disciples than the words of Jesus Himself. The Sermon on the Mount is considered by many to be the greatest recorded sermon of Jesus. This is a prime example of what I am talking about when I say that someone has a commitment doctrine. It means that they place a <u>disproportionate value on their personal commitment to the cause of Christ</u>.

To be a healthy mature Christian our worth can only be tied to the fact that God loves us, and absolutely nothing else.

Before we judge this man too harshly, let's see how much commitment doctrine is in our own lives. Have you ever thought, "I am going to be in church every time the doors are open because that is what I should do"? If we have gone to church because we should, even when we felt terrible, there is a good chance we have over-valued our commitment to God. This is not what God is expecting in our relationship with Him. We may have unknowingly tied our relationship with God to church attendance. If we miss a church service, and we feel ashamed or feel like we need a good excuse to tell everyone, we have over-emphasized our commitment to Christ. Remember Hosea 6:6, God desires mercy and the knowledge of Him more than sacrifices. This includes the sacrifices we make in order to prove our worth by keeping our commitments. **Our worth cannot be tied to our level of commitment.** To be a healthy, mature Christian our worth can only be tied to the fact that God loves us, and absolutely nothing else.

How can our own integrity be used against us?

Satan is a master at using our own integrity to destroy our relationship with God. Like Job, most people who are deceived into over-valuing their personal commitment to Christ are people of very high integrity. These are the type of people who value keeping their word at all costs. They are dependable, trustworthy, and you could build any organization better with them in it. Like Job, they are blameless, upright, fear God, and shun evil. But, their dependability will become their weakness <u>if they allow their commitment to become the measure of their worth</u>.

In most church environments where a personal relationship with God should be the most important attribute, their relationship with God will never be questioned. After all, who would dare say anything; they are the ones who are doing everything. Christians who rely on their personal relationship with God instead of their own performance will often feel a coldness from these brothers or sisters in Christ. There may be the unspoken

What is Job's Mindset?

insinuation, "What are you doing compared to me?" Focusing on our own commitment is a sign of performance-based acceptance and if others are not performing then we might look down on them as less valuable.

The reason this type of believer so admires Job is that if everything in their life fell apart, they want to believe they would stay committed just like Job. They want to be the person who does not quit at any cost because they receive the validation of their worth through their commitment. The perverted focus on commitment that Satan has been able to deceive them into following is all about <u>them</u>. It is about <u>their</u> ability to serve, <u>their</u> ability to be obedient, and <u>their</u> ability to stay the course. They would like to say what Job said, *"Though He slay me, yet will I trust Him"* (Job 13:15a). <u>This is not a healthy relationship and if we believe it is we are deceived</u>! We do not have to prove ourselves to God!

We don't have to prove our worth; God's love for us is the proof of our worth.

This is like a child who thinks that if I <u>do</u> everything daddy asks of me, if I <u>do</u> all my chores, if I <u>do</u> whatever he wants me to <u>do</u> then he will love me. Unwittingly they have been deceived into working (doing) to earn God's approval. But, what they do not realize is that they already have His approval, *"to the praise of the glory of His grace, by which <u>He made us accepted</u> in the Beloved"* (Ephesians 1:6). This is like Rachel competing with Leah to have more children for Jacob, her husband, in order to gain his love. Rachel already had the unconditional love of Jacob who had worked for her hand in marriage for seven years (Genesis 29-30). She never needed to compete with Leah. Like Rachel, we are already unconditionally loved and accepted. We don't have to prove our worth; God's love for us is the proof of our worth.

Any doctrine that causes our focus to be about us and our actions is not the heart of what God desires from our relationship. This can spill over into the songs we sing in worship when our focus should be on God. For example, the following words are from a popular hymn: "I have decided to follow Jesus...though none go with me I still will follow."[A] I am not saying these songs are evil or that they do not have value. I am only saying that we need to be careful how much we focus on our own commitment. <u>The Christian life was never meant to revolve around our ability to stay committed</u>. This is what the deception of the commitment doctrine is designed to do. Job's world revolves around himself and his actions and he doesn't even realize it.

Job has limited his relationship with God to his actions. Since he thinks it is all about his actions and he is doing all the right things, he concludes that he must have a great relationship with God. This is why God cannot get through to Job: Job is so sure he has done everything right. **Job has become trapped where he is in his spiritual journey because he has a very limited view of what a relationship with God is supposed to be.** When you get in a discussion with someone who has a mindset similar to Job, be prepared to experience the same frustration that God deals with in most of His relationships because the other party does not know they have a problem.

What is Job's limited view of his relationship with God?

In Job 28:28, Job makes a statement that he believes is from God. This gives us insight into his understanding of faith. *"And to man He said, 'Behold the fear of the Lord that is wisdom and to depart from evil is understanding'."* Job makes this statement right before the beginning of what is called his summary defense. He will afterward plead his case with God for three straight chap-

What is Job's Mindset?

ters and not speak again until God appears to him. Since Job is relying on his integrity to keep his commitment, the above verse is very significant because <u>it is the full written commitment which he believes he has been keeping</u>. The next three chapters are his final defense to prove that he kept this commitment. Please read Job's statement of faith (Job 28:28) again slowly, and answer this question. Is it true? It sounds good but, by comparing it to other scripture, we see that it is incomplete.

Because God says that Job spoke without knowledge (Job 38:2), it would be wise to discount Job's early theology and find accurate theology in other parts of the Word of God. Let's look at Proverbs 9:10 as a good reference, *"The fear of the Lord <u>is the beginning of</u> wisdom, and <u>the knowledge of the</u> Holy One <u>is understanding.</u>"* The word <u>beginning</u> here means opening or commencement. This is a very clear distinction from what Job believed to be true. Instead of fearing or reverencing God as a beginning point to wisdom, Job considered fearing God to be the total of wisdom. He also believes that by departing from evil, he has arrived at complete understanding. However, God says that knowing Him is understanding. Job is definitely motivated by an understanding of God that is woefully incomplete compared to God's word. Although Job 28:28 sounds good, it is wrong.

Using the definition of understanding in Proverbs 9:10, does Job have understanding? God's words declare that only people who know Him have understanding, but Job is ignorant of God's true character. Job knows about God the same way I know about many famous movie stars. I do not know what these people are like personally, so I cannot truthfully say that I know them. Job knows a version of God that he has made up in his mind Who is like the pagan gods that are worshipped around him. Job has transferred this faulty version of God onto the image of the one true God. Job serves his version of God the same way the pagans serve their gods by living in dread and making offerings to appease their unpredictability.

Can God be both good and bad?

An incorrect understanding of God will cause us to serve Him for the wrong reasons. Job declares something unusual about God in Job 2:10, *"...Shall we indeed accept good from God, and shall we not accept <u>adversity</u>...?"* The definition of the name <u>Satan</u> means the adversary. In this passage Job is attributing what should be understood as the work of his enemy to be the work of his God. Job's deceived view of God is one of God as both friend and enemy. He doesn't know that God is only good. This changes his motivation for serving God from one of thankfulness to one of fearful appeasement. Jesus made it perfectly clear that God is good, *"So He said to him, "Why do you call Me good? No one is good but One, that is, God"* (Matthew 19:17a). To know God is to experience His goodness; to be unaware of His goodness is to acknowledge that we have not truly known His heart.

God cannot be both good and evil or He would be working against Himself. Jesus said, *"If a kingdom is divided against itself, that kingdom cannot stand"* (Mark 3:24). Good cannot produce evil. Jesus said, *"Even so, every good tree bears good fruit, but a bad tree bears bad fruit. A good tree cannot bear bad fruit, nor can a bad tree bear good fruit"* (Matthew 7:17-18). We also find the same principle in the book of James, *"Does a spring send forth fresh water and bitter from the same opening? Can a fig tree, my brethren, bear olives, or a grapevine bear figs? Thus no spring yields both salt water and fresh"* (James 3:11-12).

What is Job's Mindset?

When we get to heaven we will not have the revelation that God was meaner than we thought!

The Lord is good: Psalm 34:8, 100:5, 106:1, 107:1, 118:1, 118:29, 135:3, 136:1, and 145:9. Every evil power is attempting to destroy your understanding of God's goodness (2 Corinthians 10:4-6). We must choose to resist any deception, no matter the source, that attempts to undermine the goodness of our God. When we get to heaven we will not have the revelation that God was meaner than we thought! We will be shocked at how little we comprehended the greatness of His love for us.

Job's regular practice was to offer sacrifices on behalf of his children after each time one of his seven sons celebrated a birthday. What compelled Job to do this? Job 1:5 says *"… For Job said, 'It may be that my sons have sinned and cursed God in their hearts.' Thus Job did regularly."* Job was sacrificing out of his fear that his children might have done something wrong toward God. His actions strongly indicate that Job was expecting repercussions if his children had indeed sinned against God. I believe, as a good father, Job was motivated to do what he could to stop those expected repercussions. Somehow this unhealthy fear of God had become rooted in Job's heart. This is not a reverential fear, but literally a dread of anticipated harm. Several translations use the word "dread" to describe Job's fear in Job 3:25.

God will not harm us in any way, and He never ties His goodness to our performance

This can be similar to how our motivation for giving can shift from a grateful heart to the fear of what God is going to do to us if we do not give. This motive can only come through a deceived understanding of the character of God. God will not harm us in any way, and He never ties His goodness to our performance. God loves us because He does, period! *"For God so loved the world that He gave..."* (John 3:16a). To dread or be terrified of what God might do to us is not the reverential respect that God wants from us. There is none of this type of fear in someone who understands God's love. 1 John 4:18 explains that the complete understanding of God's love casts out this type of fear. The evidence that Job does not understand God's love is that He still has this type of fear in his heart. This fear is motivating Job's actions.

If you are doing things for God so that He will, in return, provide ease and rest in your life, I would encourage you to stop. If it is giving, I would suggest you stop giving for a while. If it is serving, I would suggest doing nothing for a period of time. You have mistakenly fallen into the same deception as Job. Without knowing it, you are worshipping the fulfillment of an easy life more than you are worshipping God Himself. This false god will have to fall. The first commandment is, *"You shall have no other Gods before Me"* (Exodus 20:3).

If our motives are placing God in an obligatory position, then our faith is resting on our own performance and not God's love.

God will not get involved in any religious works bartering system. *"Now to him who works, the wages are not counted as grace but as debt. But to him who does not work but believes on Him who justifies the ungodly, his faith is accounted for righteousness"* (Romans 4:4-5). If our motives are placing God in an obligatory position, then our faith is resting on our own performance and not God's love. Job had made his sacrifices, therefore he expected God not to harm his children. Anyone who has put God in this position will eventually be angry with God for not meeting their expectations of compensation for their service. God can never be in our debt. Job's need to control the outcomes of his life had inadvertently caused him to bring his performance into the equation of what he deserved. This is a very common mistake among believers.

Remember, mankind was created to live in a world of peace and rest. The first thing that man did after sinning was to begin working by sewing fig leaves in an attempt to make things right again by covering their shame. This was the birth of performance-based acceptance. This was never in the heart of God as a foundation for His love, but only came into the earth after man partook from the knowledge of the tree of good and evil. This was not a restful work of trusting in our relationship with God, but a work done out of fear over the unknown consequences of sin.

The offering of sacrifices that Job is doing for his children is not done from a place of peace and rest, but from a place of anxiety. Job is trying to pacify the anger of God. However, God is not angry with Job, He loves Job. God wants a relationship with Job based on mutual understanding not fear, but Job's desire to be accepted based on his works is getting in the way of this relationship. *"For I desire mercy, and not sacrifice, <u>and the knowledge of God</u> more than burnt offerings"* (Hosea 6:6).

How does an unpredictable God affect Job's desire for rest?

Job's belief in an unpredictable God only exacerbated his longing for rest. I explained earlier that one of our strongest human desires is for things to go well or, stated differently, that we have peace and rest in our lives. We saw this as a driving factor motivating Job. Job's anxiety, caused from believing in an unpredictable deity, is enough to suck the enjoyment out of all the blessings God has showered on his life. No matter what Job does he cannot be sure of what his God will do, so he lives his life in an anxious foreboding of what is in his future.

Job chapter three is devoted to Job regretting that he was ever born. He even envies the dead because, at the very least, they have rest. *"For now I would have lain still and been quiet, I would have been asleep **(dead)**; then I would have been at rest **(dead)**"* (Job 3:13 emphasis added). *"There the wicked cease from troubling, and the weary are at rest **(dead)**. There the prisoners rest **(dead)** together; they do not hear the voice of the oppressor"* (Job 3:17-18 emphasis added). An unpredictable God throws a wrench into the possibility of achieving rest in this life. The only way Job could think of to overcome the tragedies he believes were inflicted on him by a schizophrenic God was his own death. This proves again how certain Job was that God was the source of his troubles.

To further emphasize that we are all more like Job than we realize, I will give some additional examples of how the desire for rest affects our everyday lives. A lot of people have great anticipation as they look forward to their retirement. But, what are they anticipating: rest from their work. Here is a great example. If you were to ask someone after work, "How did your day go?" almost everyone's response will be based on whether their day was easy or not. Our response will be something like: "it went like clockwork" or "it was smooth sailing". These are both references to something that is <u>easy</u> and dependable. One of my students came up with a very powerful example. We sometimes refer to a baby with this statement, "She is such a good baby". What we mean by "good" is that she is <u>easy</u> for us to deal with and does not cause us much <u>inconvenience</u>. In other words, she does not disturb our <u>rest</u>.

What is Job's Mindset?

There is an incredible irony with people who embrace Job's theology of blaming God for bad circumstances. The reason they are so quick to blame God is because they want an easy answer. They are not comprehending the truths God intended for them to receive from the book of Job because they have the same problem that Job had. They are desiring easy answers when the truth is "trouble comes." It is not comfortable to embrace the truth because the truth is not always what we want. But, God does make us a promise. *"And you will seek Me and find Me, when you search for Me with all your heart"* (Jeremiah 29:13). God never changes, therefore He cannot be unreliable (Malachi 3:6). But, if we have believed Him to be unreliable, then we will most likely not pursue a relationship with Him. This is no different from anyone whom we believe we cannot depend upon.

Is Job avoiding relationship by embracing sovereignty?

To believe an enemy who would like nothing more than to separate us from the love of our heavenly Father, can be a simple way of avoiding a closer relationship with God. Satan is enticing us to receive a perverted concept of sovereignty, but why do we want to believe God is responsible for bad things that happen? One of the reasons is our fear of intimacy. If I can see God first as an all-powerful sovereign this provides a buffer which prevents closeness in relationship. We see kings as high and lifted up, not as someone we could relate to personally. By embracing a version of God who is so emotionally removed that He would do us harm as well as good, we are, in effect, giving ourselves permission not to pursue a personal relationship with Him. Our own fears of rejection cause us to desire the protective barrier that a king/subject relationship provides.

God's desire is for us to know Him. At Mount Sinai God was trying to reveal Himself to all of the Israelites, but their fear got in the way. *"Then they said to Moses, 'You speak with us, and we will hear; but let not God speak with us, lest we die.' And Moses said to the people, 'Do not fear; for God has come to test you, and that His fear may be before you, so that you may not sin.' So the people stood afar off, but Moses drew near the thick darkness where God was"* (Exodus 20:19-21). <u>God never intended for Moses to be an isolated case of relationship</u>! God's heart has always been to not only deliver us out of the bondage of sin, but to bring us into a close personal relationship with Him. Fifty days after the first Passover God attempted to meet with the children of Israel on Mt. Sinai, but they were afraid. Fifty days after the fulfillment of Passover at Christ's crucifixion God initiated the closest of all relationships by sending the Holy Spirit to dwell in the hearts of every believer. God has never stopped pursuing a closer relationship with us.

As we focus our attention outward toward Jesus who removed our shame, our fear of intimacy is removed and with it our desire to blame God.

Why do we fear being close to God? Because we do not know the One Who is desiring the relationship and/or we fear we will not be able to do what He asks. If we focus on our sin, the resulting shame causes us to pull away from God just as Adam and Eve's shame caused them to hide themselves from God in the Garden of Eden. God's desire is that we focus on Jesus whom He sent to remove our shame. *"… Behold, I lay in Zion A chief cornerstone, elect, precious, and he who believes on Him <u>will by no means be put to shame</u>"* (1 Peter 2:6). *"Looking unto Jesus, the author and finisher of our faith, who for the joy that was set before Him endured the cross, <u>despising the shame</u>, and has sat down at the right hand of the throne of God"* (Hebrews 12:2). As we focus

What is Job's Mindset?

our attention outward toward Jesus who removed our shame, our inner barrier against intimacy is removed and with it our desire to blame God. Job did not know God as his loving Deliverer and his resulting attempts to cover the shame of his sin made him an easy target for Satan's deception about God's sovereignty.

[A]Singh, Sadhu Sundar, "I Have Decided to Follow Jesus." Wikipedia.com. Due to the lyrics' explicit focus on the believer's own commitment, the hymn is cited as a prime example of decision theology, emphasizing the human response rather than the action of God in giving faith. This has led to its exclusion from some hymnals. A Lutheran writer noted, "It definitely has a different meaning when we sing it than it did for the person who composed it." http://en.wikipedia.org/wiki/I_Have_Decided_to_Follow_Jesus, 19 April 2015.

CHAPTER 7

HOW CAN WE UNDERSTAND THEOLOGY THROUGH RELATIONSHIP?

How old is the concept of relationship?

Relationship is powerful. I can say that with certainty because God, who is Omnipotent (all-powerful), is Himself an eternal relationship. God exists as three Beings Who are actually One: God the Father, God the Son, and God the Holy Spirit. This group of three individual Beings, Who are God, is called the Trinity. They are individually separate, but are considered One. Relationship has always existed between the Individuals of the Trinity, therefore relationship itself is one of the very few foundational concepts which is eternal. Because relationship is within the Trinity itself, this means <u>relationship has never had a beginning and will never have an end</u>! This explains perfectly why thoughts about our relationships are some of the last we have before we die. In the moment of death temporal things lose their significance, but eternal things are magnified.

Not only were you desired, but your creation was also agreed upon!

We read in Genesis 1:26 of the consenting agreement of the Trinity in the creation of mankind, *"Then God said, "Let us make man in **Our** image. According to **Our** likeness; let them have dominion over the fish of the sea, over the birds of the air,* *and over the cattle, over all the earth and over every creeping thing that creeps over the earth"* (emphasis added). I hope it is meaningful that all three Persons of the Trinity were in agreement about your creation. No matter what lies you have ever heard to the contrary, you are not an accident. Not only were you desired, but Genesis 1:26 says that your creation was also agreed upon! Psalm 139:13-16 is a beautiful passage which affirms your importance to God, *"For You formed my inward parts; You covered me in my mother's womb. I will praise You, for I am fearfully and wonderfully made; marvelous are Your works, and that my soul knows very well. My frame was not hidden from You, when I was made in secret, and skillfully wrought in the lowest parts of the earth. Your eyes saw my substance, being yet unformed. And in Your book they all were written, the days fashioned for me, when as yet there were none of them."*

God's image is relational and we were made in His image. God longs to have a personal relationship with us, and that is why we were created in His image. We were created by a relational God to be in relationship with Him. Without relationship we are not discussing the one true God, but another god fabricated from lies we have believed. The Trinity, the very nature of God, completely destroys any lie that implies God is not relational. God has an eternal, unlimited capacity for relationship; He is always available to spend time with us.

What happened relationally when man rebelled against God?

The fall of mankind, which we read about in the book of Genesis, is really the story of the breaking of relationship between God and man. God has always chosen to exist resting in the relational dependence of the Trinity. This is because He knows there is strength in relationship. Until man's rebellion, mankind was resting in their relational dependence upon God. Once mankind chose to meet their own needs outside of their relationship with God, the relationship was forever altered. Their original relationship of dependence and rest had been changed. With their new knowledge of good and evil came shame, the enemy of dependence and rest. Mankind now feared God and hid from Him rather than coming toward Him in trust.

> *Concerning our relationship with God, independence is never a good thing!*

God could still relate to man, but mankind, in his independence, was too ashamed to relate to God. They even tried to cover up the shame of their independence with fig leaves, thereby laying the foundation of performance-based acceptance. They were now exposed to the knowledge of good and evil from which God had been trying to protect them. The knowledge of good and evil is a powerful relationship destroyer because it brings with it the doubt needed to undermine relationship. Resting in dependence upon God, which is the requirement for an abundant life, was now constantly in question. Concerning our relationship with God, independence is never a good thing! The only true rest is found in complete dependence upon God.

Why is Paul a good example of resting in relationship?

What happened when attempts were made on the life of the Apostle Paul? *"Then Jews from Antioch and Iconium came there; and having persuaded the multitudes, they stoned Paul and dragged him out of the city, supposing him to be dead. However, when the disciples gathered around him, he rose up and went into the city. And the next day he departed with Barnabas to Derbe"* (Acts 14:19-20). From this single account of persecution, and there are many others, we can be assured that Paul was <u>not</u> focused on ease and rest. So, what was the motivating factor in Paul's life? I think it was relational obedience. Near the end of his life Paul says this, *"Therefore, King Agrippa, I was not disobedient to the heavenly vision"* (Acts 26:19). Paul was resting in total dependence on God's will for his life, which meant He had to believe that God loved Him. This allowed him to follow obediently even though it cost him his life. Obeying while disregarding the cost, is an indication of complete trust. This is a natural byproduct of believing in God's love; the place of resting in our relationship with God, totally depending on His love for us.

We may rightfully revere the impact of Paul's life, but who of us would actually want to live it? Although we admire his obedience, somehow we feel we could never attain his level of perseverance in following Christ. For many of us this is a true assessment because we are not trusting in God's love as Paul was. Obeying during challenging times requires us to focus on God's love for us. The foundation of God's love is more stable than the foundation of striving to attain rest through our performance. Job had built a foundation upon trying to achieve temporal rest which is totally unstable. We must stand on the firm foundation of how much God loves us even when things do not go the way we plan.

How do we learn to rest and not fear?

Shadrach, Meshach, and Abednego spoke about this same type of dependent trust regardless of circumstances in Daniel 3:17-18, *"If that is the case, our God whom we serve is able to deliver us from the burning fiery furnace, and He will deliver us from your hand, O king. <u>But if not</u>, let it be known to you, O king, that we do not serve your gods, nor will we worship the gold image which you have set up."* Their faith in God's goodness was not based on their personal welfare, but on obedience to His perfect plan for their lives, regardless of the outcome of that plan. This kind of trust can only come from a heart level understanding of the goodness of God. Their understanding of God's goodness toward them created a genuine place of rest which raised them above the circumstances in which they found themselves.

A lack of understanding of God's love, and how much He desires to do good things for us, has resulted in Romans 8:28 being taught from a misguided perspective. *"And we know that all things work together for good to those who love God, to those who are called according to His purpose."* This passage has been used to promote the understanding that even if God did something bad to you it would be for your own good. The passage does not say that. Instead it is simply stating that God is doing everything possible to work through our life's events to give us an abundant life (John 10:10). Abundant life is only possible through a deeper relationship with God.

Romans 8:28 in no way implies that God is controlling all the events of our lives like a master puppeteer. It is only saying that God's heart of love is always working on our behalf regardless of life's events. God loves us and has a great plan for our life. His love for us will not change regardless of what comes our way. Understanding God's love will allow us to rest rather than be afraid of what might happen. Job was definitely someone who had a fearful misunderstanding of God's relationship with him. Job's fear of God had stolen the very rest he was after!

Why is David a good example of resting in relationship?

We have already seen how David's relationship with God compares to Job's, but we have not looked at how David reacted when circumstances did not go his way. David was anointed by God's prophet Samuel at an early age to be the king of Israel (1 Samuel 16:13), but it was a long time before He would receive his kingship. David went through much hardship before He became King. His respected mentor and current king, Saul, attempted to kill him (1 Samuel 18:11). David reacted by dodging Saul's spear while continuing to be respectful. There is no indication that David blamed God for this attempt on his life.

Saul soon became a constant enemy, even sending assassins to kill David (1 Samuel 19:11) causing David to live in a constant state of running for his life (1 Samuel 19:18). David resorted to living in caves in order to hide from his former friend, Saul (1 Samuel 22:1). In many of David's psalms, he asks God to deliver him from his enemies, but he does not blame God for the evil that is coming against him. <u>David had ample opportunity to blame God, but he apparently never considered that God could have been the source of his hardships</u>. This is because David knew God loved him and would never do such a thing.

There is one account in David's life during this period in which he fails to rest in dependence upon God. It is when he is personally disrespected by a landowner named Nabal. David's men have graciously been protecting Nabel's flocks without charge, but Nabel refused to give them even a small gift of thanks. David was so offended at Nabal that he planned to kill him (1 Samuel 25:17). Being such a man of honor himself, disrespect easily lured David away from resting in dependence upon God.

God graciously saves David from his foolishness by sending Abigail, Nabal's wife, as His spokesperson. David heeds her God inspired words and is saved from his impetuous actions. 1 Samuel 25:32-33, *"Then David said to Abigail: Blessed is the Lord God* *of Israel, who sent you this day to meet me! And blessed is your advice and blessed are you, because you have kept me this day from coming to bloodshed and <u>from avenging myself with my own hand</u>.*" David, for a moment, had forgotten Who was in charge of his life. This caused him to abandon his place of resting in God, but He quickly realized his mistake.

How does relationship triumph over the law?

I want to give you what I consider to be one of the most amazing examples of relationship that I have ever seen. I am going to show you where Jesus Himself uses the illegal actions of David to defend the actions of His own disciples. The story is recorded in Matthew 12:1-8. *"At that time Jesus went through the grainfields on the Sabbath. And His disciples were hungry, and began to pluck heads of grain and to eat. And when the Pharisees saw it, they said to Him, 'Look, your disciples are doing what is not lawful to do on the Sabbath'"* (Matthew 12:1-2).

What happens next is mind-blowing. Jesus uses the illegal actions of David as a defense for His Own disciple's actions. By using David as an example, Jesus paid him an incredible compliment. *"But He said to them, 'Have you not read what David did when he was hungry, he and those who were with him: how he entered the house of God and ate the showbread which <u>was not lawful for him to eat</u>, nor for those who were with him, but only for the priests? Or have you not read in the law that on the Sabbath the priest in the temple profane the Sabbath, and are blameless? Yet I say to you that in this place there is One greater than the temple. But if you had known what this means, 'I desire mercy and not sacrifice,' you would not have condemned the guiltless. For the Son of Man is Lord even of the Sabbath"* (Matthew 12:3-8).

CAN I TRUST GOD

The closer we grow in relationship with God the more the law seems like an enemy of that relationship.

In this account, David and his men take the holy bread from the tabernacle because they are hungry. Can this be right? If the Son of God says it is right, then it must be right! Jesus just declared emphatically that relationship triumphs over the law! Jesus is vindicating David and His own disciples for their accurate understanding of God. They believed God loved them and would want them fed over and above any law and Jesus is affirming that belief! He is using David as an example of the proper understanding of the heart of His Father. The closer we grow in relationship with God the more the law seems like an enemy of that relationship. Notice the disciples were not worried about condemnation coming from Jesus for breaking the Sabbath. *"The law of the Spirit of Life in Christ Jesus has made me free from the law of sin and death"* (Romans 8:2).

David understood what many born again believers still do not comprehend. God loves us above anything that we can do for him. He loves us above any law. David had no fear of eating bread reserved only for the priests. David's relationship with God was a <u>living</u> relationship where both parties involved knew each other, therefore David operated in <u>power</u>. *"For the word of God is <u>living</u> and <u>powerful</u>, and sharper than any two-edged sword, piercing even to the division of soul and spirit, and of joints and marrow, and is a discerner of the thoughts and intents of the heart"* (Hebrews 4:12).

God's covenant of relationship through Christ towers over the law, just as David towered over a nine foot giant once he was on his back.

David knows that God does not eat bread, but as a human being, he does. He also knows, without any doubt, his Heavenly

How Can We Understand Theology Through Relationship?

Father would not want him or his men to starve. When you know your God you are free. *"Let me be clear, the Anointed One has set us free — not partially, but completely and wonderfully free! We must always cherish this truth and stubbornly refuse to go back into the bondage of our past!"* (Galatians 1:5 TPT). When you are in a vibrant relationship with God, His words are in you. *"Your word I have hidden in my heart, that I might not sin against You!"* (Psalm 119:11). Notice it does not say that I might not sin against Your law. This is because God's covenant of relationship through Christ towers over the law, just as David towered over a nine foot giant once he was on his back. Goliath was put on his back through the power of relationship with God, not the power of the written law.

How does relationship triumph over dispensation?

Some of the theological arguments that people have raised to defend what happens in the book of Job have centered on the time period (dispensation) in which Job lived. Statements are made such as: "This was the Old Testament and God could not intervene;" or "This was before Christ came, so Satan's power had not been broken." Rather than debate these arguments let me point out that there is something that supersedes these theological debates: relationship! Why does the authority of relationship usurp the perceived authority of a dispensation? It is because God is an eternal, all-powerful relationship. **When we enter into a dependent relationship with God, there is nothing more powerful than this.**

There is overwhelming evidence that trusting in God works regardless of the time period in which we live. Moses raised a rod in his hand and split the Red Sea. How could this have been possible before Christ's coming to earth? The one word answer is: faith. Faith is nothing more than trusting in God. Sarah had a child when she was ninety years old through faith in God (Hebrews 11:11). David killed Goliath as a youth through faith in God. There are many more examples of people working from their Old Covenant revelation of God doing amazing exploits by exercising their trust in God. Faith is powerful because it is relational. When we put our trust in a God of love, that relationship triumphs over all other obstacles in its path.

What is God's easy yoke and light burden?

To give further insight into the concept of resting upon your relationship with God, I would like to share a revelation God gave me on Matthew 11:28-30. *"Come to Me, all you who labor and are heavy laden, and I will give you rest. Take My yoke upon you and learn from Me, for I am gentle and lowly in heart, and you will find rest for your souls. For My yoke is easy and My burden is light."* I was confused about the phrase "burden is light" because life can often feel very heavy. As I brought my confusion to God He said to me, "burden of command". As soon as I heard this thought, I immediately understood the simple revelation God was sharing with me.

If you find yourself stressed and anxious, check to see if you may have taken back the responsibility of running your own life.

The term burden of command is given to describe the weight of responsibility that a military leader feels over the lives of those under his command. Assuming responsibility for the lives of others is a heavy burden. God was trying to clarify to me that His yoke is supposed to be easy and His burden is supposed to be light because I am no longer to be the one who is in command of my own life. With Jesus as <u>Lord</u>, I should no longer have the

How Can We Understand Theology Through Relationship?

burden of responsibility for my life. I am just a soldier taking orders from my superior officer. Once I have fully relinquished the burden of command, my life should be much easier without the weight of its responsibility.

If you find yourself stressed and anxious, check to see if you may have taken back the responsibility of running your own life. Relinquish that responsibility to the Lord Jesus and rest in His ability to lead. You are not meant to handle the burden of responsibility for your own life. Jesus, alone, is the One capable of managing that responsibility. As one under God's authority, your yoke should be easy and your burden should be light.

God does not want to run our lives because He is not a dictatorial tyrant. However, our very limited view of God and His good plans for our life can easily be distorted by an enemy who is constantly twisting His motives. We need God to assume the burden of commanding our life because we can easily be deceived. Jeremiah 17:9 says, *"The heart is deceitful above all things, and desperately wicked; who can know it?"* Job is definitely someone who has been deceived about the goodness of God. This has caused Job's heart to distrust God, thereby causing him to resort to the familiar path of trusting himself instead.

Once Job actually sees his heavenly Father, he is free. This is because he could not look on Love and not be changed. Job now has the clear understanding that his acceptance is not based on his performance. He finally understands that God loves him, period! For the first time in his life Job is free! He is not afraid any more. *"There is no fear in love; but perfect love casts out fear…"* (1 John 4:18a). **Job finally finds his rest when he sees the goodness of God.** *"I have heard of You by the hearing of the ear, But now my eye sees You"* (Job 42:5). <u>We can never have rest if we are afraid of God</u>!

How easy is it to trust in ourselves?

We were all created with the relational need for an unchanging, dependable heavenly Father. If God's dependability is in doubt, we will find solace somewhere else we believe is more dependable. Financial blessings can often replace God by filling our instilled need for a trusting dependent relationship. We must remember that Job is one of the richest men in the world and with wealth comes multiplied responsibilities. How could Job's misunderstanding of God's goodness have altered his handling of these responsibilities? Job appears to have taken comfort by trusting in himself. In Job 29:14 Job says, *"I put on righteousness, and it clothed me; My justice was like a robe and a turban."* Job was definitely resting in his own righteousness. The young man Elihu confronts Job about his self-righteousness, *"Do you (Job) think this is right? Do you say, 'My righteousness is more than God's'?"* (Job 35:2). Before we judge Job too harshly, it is important to test our own hearts for any unhealthy dependence upon ourselves.

It is very easy for a responsible person to become deceived into trusting themselves. They often say things like, "Well, if I don't do it then who will?" This is definitely not a place of waiting on the Lord to lead. It is an indication of someone who has not learned what it means to rest in their relationship with God by depending on His leading. This attitude may come from an incorrect belief that we have been rejected or abandoned by God. The truth is that sin produces shame and shame leads us to believe there is a breakdown in our relationship with God. God has never stopped loving us regardless of our actions. Our shame makes us believe that He has, but that is a lie!

Everything Jesus suffered was for one purpose: to get you back!

How Can We Understand Theology Through Relationship?

God has not abandoned or rejected us, but has done everything possible to restore our relationship with Him. In His statement, *"….It is finished…"* (John 19:30), Jesus announced to all that He had completed His mission of destroying the *"…works of the devil"* spoken of in 1 John 3:8. The problem is, we still believe the lie that it has not been done. <u>The destruction of the power of sin was simply God's means to an end: the restoration of our relationship with Him</u>. Everything Jesus suffered was for one purpose: to get you back!

True rest can only come as we go back to the place where we were created to live. This is the place of dependence upon our relationship with God, not the place of independence that sin brought with it into our world. When we lay the burden of our lives on the gigantic shoulders of our heavenly Father, we can experience the childlike trust we were created to thrive under. Jesus spoke about this childlike trust in Luke 18:17, *"Assuredly, I say to you, whoever does not receive the kingdom of God as a little child will by no means enter it."* Being under the benevolence of a loving heavenly Father is to rest in His leadership over us.

How do we keep a proper perspective?

Jesus Christ suffered miserably and died to destroy the barrier which kept us from relationship with God. This is the greatest act of love that has ever been seen in all of human history. Depending on our age, we will live another twenty to ninety years and then we will die. If we have accepted Jesus as our Lord and Savior, even after our death, we will continue to live forever with God. Our entire lifetime on this earth is but a tiny blip compared to our eternal existence. So, how is it possible that we are able to get so angry over something as simple as a flat tire or a late bill? How can we believe that God does not care about us? Compared to our eternal relationship with God, this kind of thinking reveals a huge loss of perspective.

> **The knowledge of how much God loves us makes us determined to live the life that God gave us despite the obstacles.**

If we could draw a forever line for our lives, and were to draw a line representing the time we were having tire trouble, there would be no comparison between their respective lengths. God loves us and unequivocally demonstrated this love at the cross. People like Paul, who embraced that love, had a realistic perspective of their relationship with God. Almost anything can come against them, yet they just keep going. Paul was thrown in prison and he sang; he was beaten up and continued to the next town; he was killed and he got back up (2 Corinthians 11:23). The knowledge of how much God loves us makes us determined to live the life that God gave us despite the obstacles. It causes us to resist our true enemies. God's love gives us a shield against all of the lies that are coming against us. Embracing the relationship of True Love will cause us to live a life without fear.

CHAPTER 8

WHAT IS TRUE REST?

How is Hebrews a book about rest?

I believe the book of the Bible which has the most in common with the book of Job is Hebrews. Hebrews was written to encourage the early believers not to give up, but to press on into the true rest of God. Most of the early Christians were Jews who had stepped out of the legalism of Judaism into the grace of Christianity. Hebrews was written to those believers who would have been tempted to revert back to the <u>easier</u> life of traditional Judaism which would have provided <u>rest</u> from the persecution of their fellow Jews.

The writer of Hebrews encourages them that there is more to be gained in Christ than taking the easy way out in order to avoid persecution. These early believers were facing prison, seizure of property, and even death. Anyone of us in this situation would have had an overwhelming desire for relief or <u>rest</u>. Hebrews uses the rebellious first generation from the Egyptian exodus as examples of those who did not trust God. The book also lists all of the great Hebrew patriarchs in chapter eleven as examples of those who trusted God. The temptation to go back to their familiar laws and traditions in order to avoid persecution would have appealed to these early believers' natural desire for life to go well.

Why should our motive for pursuing God be relationship?

I would like for us to take a look at chapters three and four of Hebrews because this is where the writer focuses on the topic of rest. Hebrews 3:7-11 is a quote from Psalm 95:7b-11, *"Therefore, as the Holy Spirit says: Today, if you will hear His voice, Do not harden your hearts as in the rebellion, In the day of trial in the wilderness, Where your fathers tested Me, tried Me, And saw My works forty years. Therefore I was angry with that generation, And said, 'They <u>always go astray in their heart</u>, And <u>they have not known My ways</u>.' So, I swore in My wrath, 'They shall not enter My rest'."* In verse ten it tells us the reason they did not enter God's rest: "They always go astray in their heart." But, why did they go astray? The answer: "They have not known My ways."

Pursuing God in order to actually know Him, is the only way to receive a revelation of Who He really is.

I would like to show you a similar mention of the phrase "known His ways" which is found in a praise psalm of David, Psalm 103:7, *"He made known His <u>ways</u> to Moses, His <u>acts</u> to the children of Israel."* During this song of praise, as he is led by the Holy Spirit, David suddenly shifts the focus from praise to include verse seven. This verse gives us insight into the huge difference in Moses's relationship with God compared to the children of Israel. God showed Moses His <u>ways</u>, meaning His mode of action or motivation. Moses's kinsmen only saw God's <u>acts</u>, meaning His exploits or actions. Because Moses was pursuing God, God revealed the motivations of His heart to His friend, Moses. The children of Israel were content beholding the miraculous manifestations of God and were not interested in pursuing a relationship of the heart. Pursuing God in order to actually know Him, is the only way to receive a revelation of Who He really is.

God's actions included the ten plagues He used to expedite Pharaoh's release of the children of Israel. God also manifested a cloud to lead them by day and a pillar of fire to lead them by night. Notice that even the non-covenant Egyptians saw the acts of God. Similarly, the Sun comes up in the east and sets in the west, providing life and nourishment to all. This is an act of God and anyone can experience an act. A "way" is different because it is the motivation behind the action itself or the reason someone does what they do. Our motivation for doing something reveals our character. I believe only seeing God's actions is similar to the mental assent spoken of in James 2:19, *"You believe that there is one God. You do well. Even the demons believe—and tremble!"* God desires a much deeper relationship. He wants us to know His heart, not merely the observation of His actions.

God revealed His heart to Moses because Moses was His friend. God in essence was telling Moses, I am parting the Red Sea because I want to redeem my people. At the same time I want to destroy their enemies so that they will know that I am greater than any enemy which they will ever face. Most of the Israelites had not taken the time to know the character of the God of love; they only knew what He did. This should explain why they were murmuring and complaining only three days after coming through the Red Sea on dry land. Without knowing God's heart they were unable to trust Him.

We were made for relational dependence upon God; without it there is no rest.

Many of us think that if we could only see a miracle we would never have trouble believing God again. The Israelites walked through walls of water and saw all of their enemies destroyed in a moment. In their excitement they sang a praise song about the victory God had brought on their behalf. Yet, they were very quickly complaining against God. To me this illustrates just how important it is to know God Himself, and not just be wowed by what He can do. Learn to pursue God to find out <u>why</u> He is doing something and go the extra relational step to discover His motives.

Job did not know the heart of his God and that is a very vulnerable place. In the book of Job, God rectifies this problem in Job's life by appearing to him. One thing that we know with absolute certainty is: God loves Job. God is love (1 John 4:16) therefore, God loves Job. Without truly knowing the heart of God, Job cannot have true <u>rest</u>. We were made for relational dependence upon God, without it there is no legitimate rest.

What rest is Hebrews talking about?

The word <u>rest</u> in Hebrews means reposing down; abode, -rest. But, what does this mean practically? Hebrews 4:2-3a gives us the answer, *"For indeed the gospel was preached to us as well as to them; but the word which they heard did not profit them, <u>not being mixed with faith</u> in those who heard it. <u>For we who have believed do enter that rest</u>."* Rest, according to Hebrews is solely dependent upon trusting God. What do you believe about God? If you believe God loves you to the extent that he would sacrifice His Son in your place, then you can enter into a relationship of trusting Him. This is the rest of God.

Our desire for ease and comfort is <u>in conflict</u> with God's true rest of trusting Him.

The kind of trust that <u>rests</u> in the goodness of God is powerful. Beginning in the second chapter of Acts, we find the record of how 120 people, with this kind of trust, changed the course of history. But, if their hearts had been based on circumstances going well, it would have been a different story. For many of them, after choosing to follow Christ, life did not go well. Our desire for ease and comfort is <u>in conflict</u> with God's true rest of trusting Him. Job is no different than any of us and is used as an example of what can happen when this desire for ease becomes a false god in our lives. This desire for rest is enormous and affects us all on an almost daily basis. The only way to enter the true rest of God is by believing that God is good and has our best interest at heart. In short, the only way to enter God's rest is to trust God regardless of our personal circumstances.

What is the root cause of disobedience?

Unbelief is the root cause of disobedience. Hebrews 4:2 clearly states that a lack of faith caused the children of Israel not to enter into God's rest, *"...not being mixed with faith in those who heard it."* But, what is the root of unbelief? Is it not a lack of trust? If an earthly father commands us to do something, we do not instinctively believe that what he is telling us is for our own good. This is especially true if we are motivated by the fear of how we might be punished if we do not obey. An unexplained doubt about God's motives seems to pre-date man's rebellion against God. This uncertainty had to be present in Adam and Eve before they rebelled. What other explanation is there to explain why they doubted God so quickly, having never witnessed anything but His goodness?

It is easy for us to circumvent trust by dutifully performing what we are told to do. This is the mindset of a servant, not a son.

A lack of trust is the motivator for disobedience. God desires obedience, but not Job's type of obedience which was based on dread. God is after the type of obedience David had. God is not legalistic; He is not after obedience for obedience's sake. God is after obedience based on a trusting relationship. What happened with Job often happens with us. We may find ourselves mistakenly serving God out of duty rather than out of the relationship He longs to have with us.

Here again, we see that God's commendation of Job had little to do with their relationship, but focused on Job's performance. *"...Have you considered My servant Job, that there is none like him on the earth, a blameless and upright man, one who fears God and shuns evil?"* (Job 1:8). Job is doing everything right except the most important thing: pursuing a relationship with God. God wants the relationship to be first and the accompanying actions to come from the trust inherent in that relationship. It is easy for us to circumvent trust by dutifully performing what we are told to do. This is the mindset of a servant, not a son.

Why did God institute a Sabbath rest?

If God's true desire is trust, then what was His relational reason for instituting the Sabbath as a day of rest? Hebrews 4:4 says, *"For He has spoken in a certain place of the seventh day in this way: 'And God rested on the seventh day from all His works'"*. Now, why would God rest from His labors on the seventh day? It could not have been because He was tired, so there must have been another reason. <u>The Sabbath was instituted by God to be a day of trust</u>. By not laboring to provide for ourselves on the seventh day we are openly declaring that we trust or rest in God's provision for us and not our own ability. The Sabbath is a day of rest because it is a day of demonstrating our trust in God.

The evidence of our rest, trust, or faith in God is to cease from trying to do things on our own.

We live in such a blessed society that we sometimes fail to see the link between resting and trusting. God provides for the needs of many of us in five days or less. In an agrarian society, when you have to plant seeds and harvest crops at certain times, the decision not to work every seventh day was a much bigger deal than it is in our modern society. What is God demonstrating through instituting the Sabbath? God is boldly saying, "You can trust Me!" What is the evidence of faith? *"For he who has entered His rest has himself also ceased from his works as God did from His"* (Hebrews 4:10). The evidence of our rest, trust, or faith in God is to cease from trying to do things on our own. Now that we are in relationship we realize the truth that we were never on our own. We realize that God loves us and has always been taking care of us.

Do not take what I am about to say as an excuse for laziness. We do not have as much to do with the outcome of our lives as we think we do! We can enter into an amazing life of rest when we realize that God is working things for our good, and the outcome is not all up to us. By understanding God's love for us, we can stop striving to make things happen. When we stop striving, we have gotten out of God's way which allows Him the most freedom to work on our behalf. Job, like many of us, was not at rest. Job was carrying the burden of responsibility for the outcome of his own life.

Can someone have faith without rest?

If the evidence of true faith or resting in God is to cease from your own works, then did Job have faith? Hebrews 11:1 says, *"Now faith is the substance of things hoped for, the evidence of things not seen."* To have Biblical faith someone must have hope. Did Job have hope? *"For I know that my Redeemer lives, And He shall stand at last on the earth; and after my skin is destroyed, this I know, That in my flesh I shall see God"* (Job 19:25-26). Job did have hope, but only for the afterlife. Sadly, this is the only hope that many Christians have. This cannot be the same faith that Jesus speaks of which moves mountains, heals the sick, and raises the dead. All of these things take place <u>in this life</u>, not in the afterlife. We must have faith that trusts in God to overcome in this life. There will be no need for faith in eternity because our hope will already be fulfilled.

Without being able to enter into the rest of trusting in the goodness of God there is no real hope and, as a result, no close, personal relationship.

Job is inadvertently confessing here that his only hope is in the afterlife where he knows he does not have a part to play in the outcome. Without realizing it, Job is revealing his core belief that his life on this earth is <u>solely his responsibility</u> and is determined by his own actions or works. Without being able to enter into the rest of trusting in the goodness of God there is no real hope and, as a result, no close, personal relationship. This is another reason why Job is not mentioned in the hall of faith in Hebrews eleven. Job is trusting in himself, not in God.

Before we judge Job too harshly, we must all evaluate ourselves to see whether our hope is in our own abilities. We can easily say we are not hoping in ourselves until our world starts to fall apart. When things go badly, that is when our hearts are truly exposed. How do we react when we fail? This is a clear sign whether or not we have been hoping in our own abilities. If we find it very difficult to forgive ourselves when we fail, then we have placed our hope in our own performance and not in God. When we fail, we should forgive ourselves quickly because our hope is not in our ability it is in the finished work of Christ done on our behalf.

What is True Rest?

God was always there waiting for Job to respond to His friendship. This is evidenced by how Job's story was chosen to be included in the Bible. As we have seen there are many reasons the story of Job is included in God's word, but one of them will amaze you. Job prayed for his story to be recorded, *"Oh, that my words were written! Oh, that they were inscribed in a book!"* (Job 19:23). This might be the perfect example of that old cliché, "Be careful what you pray for." If God was faithful to answer this flippant prayer of Job, just imagine what He would have been able to do if Job had called on Him for deliverance?

What does thankfulness have to do with rest?

I have a revealing question for you. Was Job thankful? We saw earlier in chapter four that Job was anticipating bad things from God, *"… Shall we indeed accept good from God, and <u>shall we not accept adversity</u>…"* (Job 2:10). Job's motivation for sacrificing to God was to appease what he considered to be God's unpredictable nature. However, Psalm 107:21-22 says, *"Oh, that men would give thanks to the LORD for His goodness, and for His wonderful works to the children of men! <u>Let them sacrifice the sacrifices of thanksgiving</u>, and declare His works with rejoicing."* Sacrifices were intended to instill gratefulness and were meant to be given from a heart of thankfulness for the abundance that God had already provided.

Is Job sacrificing with the motivation of a grateful heart? There is no clear evidence in the book of Job that he has a thankful heart. But, how can someone who has been so blessed not have a grateful heart? Psalm 4:5 gives us the answer, *"Offer the sacrifices of righteousness, And <u>put your trust in the LORD</u>."* This psalm says that righteous or Godly sacrifices are to be given from the core motivation of trust. Now we are back to the problem in Job's heart: trust. How can he trust a God he believes will do him harm as well as good? The truth is that he can't and neither can we. This is the reason Satan has chosen to propagate Job's deceived understanding from Job 1:21, *"...The Lord gave, and the Lord has taken away...."* If we believe this, then it is impossible to completely trust God.

People who teach Job from a religious perspective try to make Job seem awesome. The reason is, from a religious standpoint, he is. Job is the poster child for doing what he is told to do because he is supposed to do it. But, this is not even close to doing something from a trusting heart. David completely understands this, *"For You do not desire sacrifice, or else I would give it; You do not delight in burnt offering. The sacrifices of God are <u>a broken spirit</u>, <u>A broken and a contrite heart</u>—These, O God, You will not despise"* (Psalm 51:16-17). David understands that the sacrifice God is really after is a humble submitted heart. David is the poster child for doing what he is supposed to do because he trusts his God and loves doing it.

What does God consider to be most important?

In Mark 12:28 one of the scribes asks Jesus what is the first commandment and Jesus replies, *"The first of all the commandments is: 'Hear, O Israel, the LORD our God, the LORD is one. And you shall love the LORD your God with all your heart, with all your soul, with all your mind, and with all your strength. This is the first commandment. And the second, like it, is this: You shall love your neighbor as yourself. There is no other commandment greater than these'"* (Mark 12: 29-31).

God loves us apart from our works! Until we understand this we will always be working to earn His approval.

What is True Rest?

This is the scribe's reply, *"…Well said, Teacher. You have spoken the truth, for there is one God, and there is no other but He. And to love Him with all the heart, with all the understanding, with all the soul, and with all the strength, and to love one's neighbor as oneself, <u>is more than all the whole burnt offerings and sacrifices</u>"* (Mark 12:32-33). This sounds exactly like David's understanding from Psalm 51:16-17. The significance of what these men have discovered cannot be over emphasized. **God loves us apart from our works!** Until we understand this, we will always be working to earn His approval. The truth is, you already have God's approval.

Listen to Jesus's reply to this scribe's understanding, *"…You are not far from the kingdom of God"* (Mark 12:34). To enter into the kingdom of God requires us to abandon our reliance upon our own works. Does this sound familiar? It should, because it takes us back to our subject of rest, *"For he who has entered His rest has himself also ceased from his works as God did from His"* (Hebrews 4:10). God wants to bring Job closer to Himself, but the obstacle of Job's reliance on his own works must first be overcome.

Jesus is the answer for all of the works (sacrifices) that need to be done for God. *"For it is not possible that the blood of bulls and goats could take away sins. Therefore, when He came into the world, He said: "<u>Sacrifice and offering You did not desire</u>, But a body You have prepared for Me. <u>In burnt offerings and sacrifices for sin You had no pleasure</u>. Then I said, 'Behold, I have come—In the volume of the book it is written of Me—To do Your will, O God'"* (Hebrews 10:4-7). Jesus's obedience, out of love for us, fulfilled all of our works. We are to rest in His finished work, trusting in God's love for us. As we saw earlier, the Apostle Paul had this same trust-based obedience born out of his understanding of God's love. Paul's rest in the heart of God allowed him to endure difficulty without blaming God!

Does Job have a pride issue?

Psalm 51:17 says, *"The sacrifices of God are <u>a broken</u> <u>spirit</u>, A <u>broken and a contrite heart</u>—These, O God, You will not despise."* What is a broken spirit and what is a broken and contrite heart? The word for <u>broken</u> means to crush, break, or be broken. And the word <u>spirit</u> is referring to the spirit part of man, not to the indwelling Holy Spirit that we receive after salvation. This verse is telling us that our human spirit needs to be humbled. We need to do away with our ego and the pride of thinking we are the most qualified person to control our own life. We desperately need to submit to the Lordship of Jesus.

Anxiety is a result of us being in charge!

Once we have released the control of attempting to run our own life, then we should feel the peace of leaning on the Lord despite the circumstances. Our natural tendency is to believe that our peace is dependent upon circumstances, but true peace is solely dependent upon trusting God. Many of us have that peace initially when we are first saved, but over time circumstances may arise that cause us to take back the responsibility for our own well-being. This is the cause of much of the anxiety that we deal with as Christians. Anxiety is a result of us being in charge!

We are commanded in Philippians 4:6, *"<u>Be anxious for nothing</u>, but in everything by prayer and supplication, with thanksgiving, let your requests be made known to God."* The result of trusting God fully for everything we desire is given in the next verse, *"<u>And the peace of God</u>, which surpasses all understanding, will guard your hearts and minds through Christ Jesus"* (Philippians 4:7). We must purposely choose to put the most qualified Leader back in charge of our lives, and only then can we experience the true rest and peace of God in our lives again. With Job's misunderstanding of God's character, God was his master, but not his trusted Leader.

God needs our broken spirit as a sacrifice so that He is able to work in our life unhindered.

Job does not immediately seem to have an issue with pride, but it is there. For someone to not fully relinquish control to God's leadership of their life, after claiming Him as their Lord, is an indication they believe they are smarter than God. None of us would ever openly say that we are smarter than God. When we consider that God is omniscient (all knowing) and we are not, what other explanation than pride could there be for taking control of our own lives? We are claiming that our limited understanding of what is going on makes us more qualified to make a decision than the One Who knows everything. I realize that we may have been driven to this point through fear or some other attack against us, but this is still a sign of arrogance. Pride causes us to take charge and that's why we need to be put back in our place—we are not the leader.

God needs our broken spirit as a sacrifice so that He is able to work in our life unhindered. This is not because He has a thirst for power, but because He desires to bless us and our pride gets in His way. There cannot be two leaders in our life. Job's pride had limited God to only being able to bless Job with earthly possessions and earthly relationships. Even though these are wonderful, God wants so much more for Job and for us as well. He wants to bless us with the abundant life that comes through experiencing the peace and rest of knowing how much He truly loves us. For God to do this He has to be the Leader. The heart knowledge of knowing how much our Heavenly Father loves us makes us whole. God longs to see Job completely whole.

Why is relinquishing leadership of our lives an ongoing decision?

We can learn much about Job by comparing the relationship he had with God to the relationship Abraham had with God. "And the Scripture was fulfilled which says, 'Abraham believed God, and it was accounted to him for righteousness.' <u>And he was called the friend of God</u>" (James 2:23). Now this is a powerful commendation. If God were introducing Abraham at a meeting He would say, "This is My friend, Abraham." Now that is a place of prominence! Remember, by contrast, God would introduce Job by saying, "This is My servant, Job." There is a big difference between being a friend and a servant. Don't let anyone try to dazzle you with how great a man of faith Job was. This comparison makes it very clear that he was not in the same category of relationship as Abraham. We saw earlier that he was not in the same category of relationship as David, whom God described as a man after His Own heart.

There is much we can learn about God's leadership of our life from Abraham's example. God was gracious enough to show us all the ups and downs in His relationship with Abraham. The downs all resulted when Abraham made the crucial mistake of taking back control of his own life. On two occasions, this friend of God allowed his wife to be taken captive by foreign kings because he feared that they might kill him. (Genesis 12:15, 20:2). Fear had caused God's friend to take back control of his own life. This almost cost him his marriage. Both times, God graciously intervened to protect His friend's marriage.

The only way to genuinely resist the temptation to take the lead in our lives comes through understanding how much God loves us.

What is True Rest?

God's promise that Abraham and Sarah would be parents had been so long in coming that Abraham lost patience. Abraham took personal responsibility for fulfilling God's promise by taking a second wife. This was his attempt to fulfill the plans of God through his own leadership (Genesis 16:3). The results were disastrous for Abraham and Sarah's marriage and also for the peace of the whole world from then until now. The descendants of Ishmael (the Arabs), who were born through Abraham's decision to take control of his own life, are still trying to kill the descendants of Isaac (the Jews) who were born according to God's plan.

Abraham had faith in God and that is why he was called a friend of God. But, like Abraham, we all face the daily decision of whether we will continually trust God to lead our lives. We all have the free will necessary to make our own autonomous decisions. God has made it clear from the life of His friend Abraham that the results of taking back our life's leadership can be disastrous. The only way to genuinely resist the temptation to take the lead in our lives comes through understanding how much God loves us. If we really know, on a heart level, His deep love for us, we will have the strength needed to trust Him even when things do not look like they will work out.

CHAPTER 9

VITAL LIFE LESSONS FROM JOB

What are God's warnings about material blessings?

Since Job was a very wealthy man, it is important that we think from his perspective as we understand some of the forces influencing him. Here are some warnings from God about material blessings. This is His warning to the Hebrew refugees who, having fled Egypt, are about to receive a huge financial windfall as they take possession of the land God has promised them. *"So it shall be, when the LORD your God brings you into the land of which He swore to your fathers, to Abraham, Isaac, and Jacob, to give you large and beautiful cities which you did not build, houses full of all good things, which you did not fill, hewn-out wells which you did not dig, vineyards and olive trees which you did not plant — when you have eaten and are full — <u>then beware, lest you forget the LORD who brought you out of the land of Egypt, from the house of bondage</u>"* (Deuteronomy 6:10-12).

We are often unaware of the present moment in which we are living because our minds are so distracted by other things. You are at this very moment reading a book in a certain environment in an exact location, but until I mentioned it to you, I doubt whether you were even conscious of your surroundings. Likewise, God has blessed us and prospered us in many ways, but if we do not consciously think about God's blessings, we will forget them. Prosperity can take care of our immediate material needs, but God warns us that once our needs are met we tend to forget where the blessings came from. Prosperity can often cause us to forget the gracious blessings of God simply because they have already been provided. Something that is already available is quickly taken for granted.

There is a further consequence of increased financial blessing: it can cause pride. *"<u>When your heart is lifted up</u>, and you forget the Lord your God who brought you out of the land of Egypt, from the house of bondage"* (Deuteronomy 8:14). But, how can prosperity cause pride? Very simply, we are easily deceived into believing that we are the ones responsible for our own financial blessing instead of being the recipients of God's love toward us. *"Then you say in your heart, '<u>My power</u> and <u>the might of my hand</u> have gained me this wealth"* (Deuteronomy 8:17). But, how do these observations relate to Job and his circumstances?

If our relationship with God is <u>not</u> based on an accurate understanding of His goodness, material possessions can often replace God as our security.

On the surface it does not appear that Job has a problem with his wealth. In God's commendation of Job we see that he fears God and shuns evil (Job 1:8). So where is the problem? When Job's rest was disturbed He told us in his own words that his biggest desire had been to maintain ease and rest by avoiding hardship (Job 3:25-26). Remember, what we fear is losing what we reverence or esteem. Job's inordinate fear of trouble is only intensified by his wealth. His material prosperity allowed him to keep a façade of security helping to mask his hidden fears.

If our relationship with God is <u>not</u> based on an accurate understanding of His goodness, material possessions can often replace God as our security. *"The name of the Lord is a strong tower; the righteous run to it and are safe. The rich man's wealth* *is his strong city, and like a high wall in his own <u>esteem</u>"* (Proverbs 18:10-11). The word <u>esteem</u> means imagination. It is very easy for us to <u>imagine</u> material possessions as our security when, in actuality, it is the God of love Who is our security and Who gave us those possessions.

> ***Only someone with an accurate understanding of God's goodness can properly balance material wealth in their life.***

It is impossible for Job not to have had difficulty dealing with His wealth because it is clear that he does not have the proper understanding of the goodness of God. Only someone with an accurate understanding of God's goodness can properly balance material wealth in their life. God loves us and wants our relationship with Him to be the place we run to for protection. God wants us to realize that He is our <u>only</u> strong tower. God did not give us what we have today so that we can trust in it for our protection; God gave us what we have because He loves us enough to provide for us.

The Apostle Paul is a great example of someone who had learned the proper place for material possessions in his relationship with God. *"Not that I speak in regard to need, for I have learned in whatever state I am, to be content: I know how to be abased, and I know how to abound. Everywhere and in all things I have learned both to be full and to be hungry, both to abound and to suffer need. I can do all things through Christ who strengthens me"* (Philippians 4:11-13). Paul's strong tower was not his possessions, it was Christ. As an unsaved Pharisee, Saul, who is later called Paul, was raised in the upper echelon of Hebrew society. Saul had known wealth, but it is only after God encounters him personally on the road to Damascus that he would have known the God of love. God provided Saul's material blessings long before Saul ever knew Him, but it is only after Saul meets God that he gains the proper perspective on wealth.

As a wealthy Pharisee, it is a very good possibility that Saul's wealth could have fueled his religious pride. Saul's mission had been to eradicate the early Christian movement which was started among the poorest in Jerusalem. In that time, the prevailing Hebrew understanding was that wealth was a sign of God's blessing. A good scriptural example would be how shocked Jesus's disciples were when He said, *"...it is hard for a rich man to enter the kingdom of heaven"* (Matthew 19:23). Their reaction speaks volumes, *"When His disciples heard it, they were greatly astonished, saying, 'Who then can be saved?'"* (Matthew 19:25).

Due to this same mindset, Saul could have felt justified in his mission to destroy this heretical Christian movement which was predominately among the poor. His justification would have been that most of its followers were lacking the validation of the financial blessing of God on their lives. After his encounter with Christ, Saul, now called Paul, would later be led by God's Spirit to write, "But God has chosen the foolish things of the world to put to shame the wise, and God has chosen the weak things of the world to put to shame the things which are mighty" (1 Corinthians 1:27). The very nature of God is to choose the most improbable people to spread His good news.

It is an extremely dangerous deception for us to measure our spirituality based upon our material possessions.

Job's wealth, like Saul's, could have mistakenly led him to believe that he was right. After all, Job was the one who had the most blessings in his life, so he naturally concluded that he must be right. This thought process is still prevalent in the church today. It is an extremely dangerous deception for us to measure our spirituality based upon our material possessions. God loves us and wants us to be aware of the dangers that can overtake our hearts if we place our security in our possessions instead of our relationship with Him.

We must test our hearts periodically concerning our material possessions to see if we have been deceived into trusting in them. Being prideful about what we have is evidence of this deception. God has clearly warned us in many places of these dangers, but it is up to us to keep a vigilant watch. Christ died for us whether we have possessions or not. If we find ourselves happy when we "do have" and sad when we "don't have" then we need to ask God to help us put the foundation of our trust back on His love for us.

How can purposely remembering help our perspective?

Let's look again at Deuteronomy 8:14, *"when your heart is lifted up, <u>and you forget</u> the Lord your God who brought you out of the land of Egypt, from the house of bondage."* We saw how pride can come from trusting in material possessions, but what about the issue of how easily we forget what God has done for us? There is something about prosperity that, if we do not consciously remember who brought it to us, we soon forget. We must purposely remember God's blessing if we are to maintain a grateful heart. <u>Once a need is met, we often immediately shift our focus to the next unfulfilled need</u>. We can spend our lives living from one need to the next without experiencing the love that God is trying to show us through His provision.

It is very easy for a responsible person to be deceived into trusting themselves and Job was a very responsible person.

CAN I TRUST GOD

I believe Job had failed to remember God's provision and this added to his misunderstanding of God's goodness. Considering the blessings God had showered on Job, if he had maintained a grateful heart, how could he possibly have blamed God for his troubles? Somewhere along the way, I believe Job started to take responsibility for his own prosperity. This is exactly what you would expect from someone who felt that God was unpredictable. It is important to remember that Job thought God could take away just as easily as He could give.

It is very easy for a responsible person to be deceived into trusting themselves and Job was a very responsible person. Since Job's perception was one of a vacillating God, then he would feel compelled to shoulder the dependability he believed God lacked. Many of us do this very same thing. If the Holy Spirit is speaking to you about this, repent and ask for His guidance on how to trust your heavenly Father more. <u>You will never be more dependable than God!</u> This is a form of self-righteousness and is a hideous deception.

> **When we chose to remember, we are receiving the maximum benefit of understanding God's love through His provision.**

As we purposely choose to focus on God's provision for us, we develop a childlike trust in a God who is always faithful. The next time we have a need, we remember more clearly how God came through for us the last time. God is constantly bringing victory in our lives; He is working to prosper us; He is building Godly relationships, but we forget that He is doing it. We are very quick to whine about what He is <u>not</u> doing for us at the moment. We must constantly fight against this natural tendency of our fallen nature by choosing to remember the many great things that God has already done for us. When we chose to remember, we are receiving the maximum benefit of understanding God's love through His provision. Because Job admits that he is living in dread of the next bad event (Job 3:25), I believe he is living from crisis to crisis, which is exactly the mindset that causes someone to quickly forget God's blessings.

What does Job's thought process teach us?

Have you ever heard this statement, "Your life <u>goes</u> the direction of your dominate thought"? Because it agrees with God's word in Proverbs 23:7a, *"For as he thinks in his heart, so is he"*, I believe the above statement to be absolutely correct. By using Job's own words I want to demonstrate the dangers of his dominant thought process. There are many verses that address Job's desire for rest. I would like to focus on Job 3:26, but this time in the King James Version, *"I was not in <u>safety</u>, neither had I rest, neither was I quiet; yet trouble came."* Notice the word "safety" which is translated "ease" in the New King James Version. I believe taken together both translations give us a clearer picture. The ease that it speaks of is from the fear of uncertainty that haunted Job's mind. <u>This explains the core problem in Job's heart: deep down he never felt safe</u>. How could he with an unpredictable, all-powerful God on the loose? The source of Job's trouble is that he does not trust God. In most of our lives this is the predominate issue as well.

This desire to be safe is even more predominate in Job's thoughts after tragedy strikes. What had been running in the background of his mind is now on display for all of us to see. I do not believe Job's primary focus was ever aquiring possessions because He never really speaks about their loss. He only mentions that God took them away (Job 1:21b). However, Job does seem to be fixated on his loss of rest. Zophar, one of Jobs friends, even tries to get Job to repent so he could have the rest he is pursuing; "<u>And you would be secure</u>, because there is hope; yes, you would dig around you, <u>and take your rest in safety</u>. You would also lie down, and <u>no one would make you afraid</u>" (Job 11:18-19a).

Your friends are usually aware of what you are afraid of, and Job's friends are not an exception. Job's friends were fully aware of his obsession for security. Their awareness of Job's fears makes me wonder if everyone around Job had a similar misunderstanding of God's character. Is everyone Job knows also afraid of God? There is a strong possibility that this is the case. In this respect the book of Job strongly emphasizes the importance of having a personal relationship with God. Everything in Job's life could have gone very differently had he known God's true character and been able to trust Him.

How far can our desire for rest lead us?

The following analogy is only intended as a means to point out the motivating factor behind most acts of abortion. If you are someone who, for whatever reason, has had an abortion, God loves you and there is complete forgiveness in Christ with no condemnation. Sin was dealt with at the cross and you can freely embrace your forgiveness through Christ. Abortion is a dramatic example of the dangers that can come from a fixation on ease and rest. To what god are aborted babies offered? Most of the time it is the god of convenience. If I built an altar and sacrificed the millions of babies that have been murdered through the act of abortion, 99% of the time the babies would have been sacrificed on the altar of convenience. Convenience is just another way of saying ease and rest.

Having an unexpected child is a very fearful proposition, and that fear can easily override trust. There is no denying that a baby will dramatically change your life. However, if our trust is in God to provide security and rest, then there can be legitimate peace and rest even during an unplanned pregnancy and the subsequent parenthood. Often times even loved ones may pressure us to take the <u>easy</u> way out so our lives can stay <u>secure</u> and our <u>rest</u> will not be disrupted. This is only evidence that the person giving the advice does not themselves trust God. **Anyone who would counsel someone to have an abortion does not trust God!** In our fallen human nature we are easily convinced to lean on our own understanding, but this is not what God's word tells us to do. *"Trust in the LORD with all your heart, and <u>lean not on your own understanding</u>; in all your ways acknowledge Him, And He shall direct your paths"* (Proverbs 3:5-6).

No one would actually come out and say, "You can't trust God." But, isn't that what they are really saying? John 10:10 says, *"The thief does not come except to steal, and to kill, and to destroy. I have come that they may have life, and that they may have it more abundantly."* God's plan for our abundant life can only happen if we trust Him. Satan's easiest theft in our lives will come when he convinces us to trust in ourselves or the advice of others more than in our heavenly Father. When we are convinced that God loves us, it is a lot easier to follow His leading above all others because we are confident that He always has our best interest at heart.

Why doesn't God just show up and tell Job He loves him?

We looked earlier at an attribute of God found in 1 Corinthians 13:4 which is love does not parade itself. This means God will not appear to us to brag about His love. Let me explain this with a question. If someone says that they love us, how do we know for sure? The answer can only be revealed through their actions. Or more accurately, what they do over an extended period of time. Have you ever heard the statement, "They're all talk."? God is the opposite of "all talk". God is all action. Jesus is God moved with compassion for you. Jesus is Love in action.

God does not show up and tell us how much He loves us because He is too busy loving us. God has been loving on Job excessively, but Job believed lies that made him think otherwise. The integrity of God will not allow Him to boast about His love. When God appears to Job He does not speak of His love, He only compares His actions with Job's in order that through comparison He might destroy Job's foundation of his own works.

Material possessions alone are not Job's greatest blessing. Job has been highly favored with ten children. Not only are there ten of them but seven of the ten are sons who will be able to work in their father's farming business. Ask any farmer how they would feel about having seven strong sons to work the land and care for the livestock. Job is one extremely blessed man. If we contrast Job's blessings with his drastic fears of impending doom, we receive further clarification as to the severity of his problem of understanding the goodness of God.

How are we to understand God's jealousy?

It is important for us to understand that God is jealous for Job. Later, when the law is given, this is the first commandment, *"You shall have no other gods before Me"* (Exodus 20:3). What was Job's idol? As we have already seen it was rest or security which is also the idol of many of us today. God's version of jealousy is very different from man's version of jealousy. Man's jealousy says, because you like someone else more than me, you are stealing from me. However, God's jealousy is not motivated from self-centeredness, but from the motive of giving. God is passionate for what is in your best interest, and your best interest is for Him to be number One in your life. Because God is Love, He wants Job to have an abundant life. God knows that Job will never be able to experience an abundant life as long as his security is placed in the false idol of rest.

God is not thinking about His own interests. According to 1 Corinthians 13:5, love does not seek its own. God is trying to get Job to the source of life which is Himself. It would be in Job's best interest to be totally dependent upon God. That is the place Job will find the true rest that his soul is longing for. God wants to give Job the desire of his heart which is legitimate rest. The only legitimate rest is total dependence upon God. The problem is that this is the same God of Whom Job is afraid.

What is the correct way to receive revelation from God's word?

God reveals Himself through relationship, so revelation leading to correct doctrine can only come through relationship.

God's word was written for us so that we might deepen our relationship with God. There is only one accurate way to receive understanding from God's word. That way is by reading it for the purpose of developing a deeper relationship with God. One of the reasons people have developed such erroneous doctrine from the book of Job is that they were studying it for the wrong reasons. Anyone who is studying God's word outside of pursuing relationship with Him will come to inaccurate conclusions from their study. If the purpose for study is solely to prove a point or solely to prove someone else is wrong, then the understanding attained will be limited or flawed. This limited understanding of God produces incorrect doctrine about God's true character. God reveals Himself through relationship, so revelation leading to correct doctrine can only come through relationship.

My focus so far has been on relationship because that is why the book of Job was written. Job's relationship with God was flawed because he was serving Him for the wrong reasons. Ironically, many of the people who acquire incorrect theology from the book of Job have a similar problem. They are not approaching the book of Job in an attempt to relate to God, but from some other motivation. The driving force behind their incorrect motives is a misunderstanding of the character of God. If you are still waiting for this book to sound more theological, you are probably the very person who needs a revelation on the character of God. God answers through relationship not through religion. If you are not sure this statement is true then look at how close Jesus was to His disciples and how those relationships have impacted the world.

What can the book of Job teach us about friendship?

Job's three friends were genuine and truly cared about Job. As time went on their attitudes toward Job became confrontational and even hostile, but I can prove that they were genuine friends. *"And when they raised their eyes from afar, and did not recognize him, they lifted their voices and <u>wept</u>; and <u>each one tore his robe and sprinkled dust on his head toward heaven</u>. So <u>they sat down with him on the ground seven days and seven nights</u>, and no one spoke a word to him, for they saw that his grief was very great."* (Job 2:12-13). How many of us have friends that would be so distraught for us that they would do these things?

Vital Life Lessons from Job

Time causes most of us to become frustrated with others when we do not see the results that we want to see in their lives.

It is often easy to become frustrated with our friends. We care, but may not know what to do. Our concern may produce a strong desire to see improvement. This can lead us to become critical which is what happened with Job's friends. Here is a practical example. While in Bible College, the husband of one of the student's had a debilitating health issue. I remember a fellow student earnestly praying for him with impassioned prayers of faith for a few weeks. After three weeks I heard this same student who had earnestly prayed for him say this, "Well, he is just going to have to learn how to believe for himself." I am not saying that there is not some truth in that statement. However, my concern is that our need to see improvement can be a stronger driving factor than our Biblical mandate for compassion.

What caused this drastic change in Job's three friends? I believe it was the frustration that comes over time. Time causes most of us to become frustrated with others when we do not see the results that we want to see in their lives. Although this response is very typical, that does not make it Godly. God does not treat us this way because He is always patient (1 Corinthians 13:4). God continues to hope all things despite what He sees (1 Corinthians 13:7). Frustration, anger, and agitation toward others can be driven by our desire to see instantaneous change in their lives.

Just as we are to trust God with the leadership of our own lives, we must trust Him with the lives of our friends.

Patience with others is definitely not a natural trait. We must be diligent to avoid the easy temptation of becoming agitated at others as Job's friends did. This agitation is activated in us when our imagined plans for others are disrupted. In other words, our vision for rest can even extend to other people. Just as we are to trust God with the leadership of our own lives, we must trust Him with the lives of our friends.

What happens when answers become our god?

Underneath the frustration over our friend's situation is our driving quest for answers. If answers are our God then we will eventually throw anyone under the bus. If we have to have answers and do not get them, we will eventually turn to blame shifting to create the explanation we so desperately need. This can even be someone who has mentored us in the ways of God. If tragedy strikes and we "try" what they taught us and it "does not work" then we blame them for being in error.

This need for answers is magnified the most when we are trying to help others through a difficult situation. How do you treat others when things are going badly in their lives? What if someone is in depression, but not praying or reading the word like you think they should? How do you treat them? Job's friends were good to him until he did not do what they expected him to do to solve his problem. Be honest, we have all done this. If it was not in person, we have all judged from a distance. We have all thought: if they would just follow my wisdom they would be fine. Behind our judgment is the need for an _easy_ answer so we can get on with our _restful_ life. Job's friends needed to get on with their lives, and Job was not listening to their "wisdom".

God is not moved by our anxious desire for answers. God is only motivated by His love for us. God died for the sinner and the righteous. He sends rain to bless everyone. To be like God we must fight against our strong desire to make sense out of every situation. We especially must resist the need to shift blame as a way of coming up with answers. We are to show compassion and be forgiving no matter the actions of the other person. This is one of the lessons God is trying to teach us through Job's friendships. This is literally one of the easiest things to talk about, but one of the hardest things to put into practice. God was very angry with Job's friends (Job 42:7). I believe it was because they had moved beyond the compassion of God to a selfish desire to have everything resolved quickly, so that they could get on with their lives.

CHAPTER 10

JOB'S CONFESSIONS OF CONFUSION

Why should we count the blessings of our time?

Before we delve into some unusual quotes from the book of Job, I do want to make a few distinctions between the time Job lived and now. Since the era of Job three major changes have taken place that should give us a better understanding of God's love. First, Jesus has died on the cross demonstrating to us the depth of God's love for us. By taking our punishment upon Himself Jesus showed us that God would do anything for our relationship. Second, we now have the written word of God which enables us to read about God's love. Third, after accepting Jesus as our Lord and Savior, God is now able to send the Holy Spirit to live on the inside of us. The Holy Spirit is our live-in instructor and He can eliminate any confusion we have about God, *"Now we have received, not the spirit of the world, but the Spirit who is from God, <u>that we might know the things</u> <u>that have been freely given to us by God</u>"* (1 Corinthians 2:12). As a Christian, God is now able to communicate directly with us, but Job was unable to enjoy any of these avenues of communication. Even as a non-believer, God still has the avenues of His written word and the death of Jesus to convey His heart of love. None of these were available to Job.

How should we fight against works-focused religion?

God is good and Satan knows he cannot withstand those who know it.

If you are going to fight a war then it would be advisable to go into battle with the most powerful weapon at your disposal. That weapon is: **the revelation of the goodness of God**. The church was built upon the rock of the revelation of God through His Son Jesus. Christ Jesus, the Anointed One, demonstrated completely the goodness of God while on earth. *"Simon Peter answered and said, 'You are the Christ, the Son of the living God.' Jesus answered and said to him, 'Blessed are you, Simon Bar-Jonah, for flesh and blood has not revealed this to you, but My Father who is in heaven. And I also say to you that you are Peter, and on this rock I will build My church, and the gates of Hades shall not prevail against it'"* (Matthew 16:16-18). God is good. Any lie to the contrary is an act of war! God is good and Satan knows he cannot withstand those who know it.

I will be emphasizing more of Job's statements to shed light on his beliefs. My hope is that by doing so we will break the power of any similar misunderstandings. The same strongholds that Job had still exist in many hearts today. Satan has used a form of religion to fortify a stronghold in the hearts of believers concerning the book of Job. He is able to achieve this in large part by inflating the feelings of respect that are so often bestowed upon Job. Satan's strategy is accomplished by magnifying God's commendation of Job, and by utilizing a few key verses while ignoring the bulk of Job's statements. Job is admired by works-focused religious people as a role model for the perfect commitment testimony: "I am so committed that whatever God does to me, I will still serve Him."

Job is not to be emulated; he is to be looked upon with compassion, just as anyone is who has been deceived.

My hope is that by bringing many of Job's inaccurate statements into the open he will no longer be used as a role model.

Job's Confessions of Confusion

Most of Job's confessions are woefully misguided. Works-focused religious people will ignore the discrepancies in the majority of Job's comments in order to find the one comment that will support their desire to emulate him. Job is not to be emulated; he is to be looked upon with compassion, just as anyone is who has been deceived. Job does not have a clue what his God is really like.

God's perfect, unchangeable character makes Him Holy and the only One Who is worthy to be worshipped. God can never change, *"For I am the LORD, I do not change"* (Malachi 3:6a). God is forever good and that is why He is the only One worthy to be worshipped. Jesus had this to say about His Father, *"…Why do you call Me good? No one is good but One, that is, God"* (Mark 10:18). <u>It would take a very confused person to continue to respect and honor someone they believed had killed their children</u>. This is further evidence that Job is very deceived. We don't worship God in spite of His character (as Job believed), but we worship God because of His character.

When did Job's heart change toward God?

Job makes an interesting comment to his friends in Job 6:14, *"To him who is afflicted, kindness should be shown by his friend, <u>even though he forsakes the fear of the Almighty</u>"*. Job speaks this out of frustration over how his friends have been treating him. Job admits that he has thrown off the fear of God. Later we will look at why he has done this, but for now I want you to see that He has done so and he knows it. Job is going through a process whereby the religious strongholds in his life are being broken. The strongholds in Job's heart had been strengthened by the acts of service he thinks he has been doing <u>for</u> God. Job is unaware that focusing on his own works has undermined his relationship <u>with</u> God. Job's performance, which had been his insurance from harm, no longer appeared to be working for him. When Job's terror of God subsides, he begins to reveal the understanding of his heart.

Job's tragedies have amplified his desire for ease and comfort.

Here is some very graphic imagery of the evil God that Job envisions in his heart. *"For the arrows of the Almighty are within me; my spirit drinks in their poison; the terrors of God are arrayed against me"* (Job 6:4). *"When I say, 'My bed will <u>comfort</u> me, My couch will <u>ease</u> my complaint, Then You scare me with dreams And terrify me with visions, So that my soul chooses strangling and death rather than my body. I loathe my life; I would not live forever. Let me alone, for my days are but a breath'"* (Job 7:13-16). Notice that Job's tragedies have amplified his desire for ease and comfort. Job's anger at God is amplified because he thinks God has destroyed his ability to have rest. There is absolutely no doubt that Job is blaming God for his problems, *"Have I sinned? What have I done to You, O watcher of men? <u>Why have You set me as Your target</u>, So that I am a burden to myself?"* (Job 7:20).

For any of us who have idolized Job, his next statements must cause us to question our understanding. Remember, this is Job speaking about God. *"…Therefore I say, '<u>He destroys the blameless</u> and the wicked. If the scourge slays suddenly, <u>He laughs at the plight of the innocent</u>. The earth is given into the hand of the wicked. <u>He covers the faces of its judges</u>. If it is not He, who else could it be?'"* (Job 9:22-24). Job says that God: destroys the blameless, laughs at the plight of the innocent, and perverts justice. We do not have to be theological geniuses to understand that Job is very confused about God's character! The last statement in Job 9:24 is very revealing, *"…If it is not He, who* *else could it be?"* Does anyone, like me, want to jump up and scream, "Job, you have an enemy, and it is not God!"?

I have made a statement before that is worth repeating. The closer you are to God, the more you know your enemies. Here is an analogy that may be helpful in explaining why. In order for someone to spot counterfeit currency they must handle the real currency a great deal. The logic is this: the more familiar they are with the real, the easier it will be to recognize the counterfeit. The closer you are to God, the more you know the real God. The more you know His character, the more you know when something is not right. The above statement of Job's is a testament to the fallacy of his knowledge of God. Job is completely unaware that he even has an enemy.

What is the deepest desire of Job's heart?

Job desires a relationship with God that is not based on fear. *"Let Him take His rod away from me, and <u>do not let dread of Him terrify me</u>. <u>Then I would speak and not fear Him</u>, But it is not so with me"* (Job 9:34-35). Job wants a relationship with God, but his terrifying fears keep him away. *"Your hands have made me and fashioned me, an intricate unity; <u>yet You would destroy me</u>"* (Job 10:8). Job knows God is his Creator, but also believes God is his destroyer. I believe Job always wanted to voice his frustration about God's mismanagement of events, but the fear of what God might do had restrained him. Now that it appears circumstances can't get any worse, Job gets honest about his feelings.

Does Job's commitment have him trapped?

Job's reliance upon his own commitment may have entangled him further in his deceptions about God. *"Though He slay me, yet will I trust Him. Even so, I will defend my own ways before Him"* (Job 13:15). The strength of Job's relationship with God is based on his own ability to stay in the relationship no matter the cost. The problem with this understanding is how prideful it is. It is all based on Job's confidence in his own abilities. The gospel is based on God's ability to stay in relationship with us. God will never be the weak link in our relationship; we all must swallow our pride and realize we are the weak link.

A pious religion develops in our hearts when we begin to take pride in our own acts of service to God. This same piety can also take pride in the performance of others whom we admire. If the understanding of anyone with this kind of attitude toward God is questioned, they may become defensive. They may also become defensive if the understanding of someone they admire is questioned. The reason some people may be offended by this book is that they could feel that I have demeaned Job, someone whom they admire. I am not demeaning Job in any way. I am only saying he is a victim of deception. I believe Job was acting in perfect agreement with the lies that he has believed.

Job's misunderstanding of God is making him feel ensnared with no way out, *"For You write bitter things against me, And make me inherit the iniquities of my youth. You put my feet in the stocks, and watch closely all my paths. You set a limit for the soles of my feet"* (Job 13:26-27). In Job's mind there can be no hope because God Himself is the problem, *"As water wears away stones, and as torrents wash away the soil of the earth; So You destroy the hope of man"* (Job 14:19). Job is saying it is God who is taking away his hope. We know from God's word that this is not possible, *"Now may the God of hope fill you with all joy and peace in believing, that you may abound in hope by the power of the Holy Spirit"* (Romans 15:13).

Job's Confessions of Confusion

Does Job's venting at God bring him relief?

"A lamp is despised in the thought of one who is at ease; It is made ready for those whose feet slip" (Job 12:5). Job is saying to his friends that because they are currently at ease they despise his need for answers. He believes this is the reason they are not comforting him the way they should. Job is envious of the fact that his friends are trouble free while he is going through a living hell.

Job's venting is not bringing him relief, *"Though I speak, my grief is not relieved; And if I remain silent, how am I eased? But now He has worn me out; You have made desolate all my company. You have shriveled me up, And it is a witness against me; My leanness rises up against me And bears witness to my face. He tears me in His wrath, and hates me; He gnashes at me with His teeth; My adversary sharpens His gaze on me"* (Job 16:6-9). Job is saying that God is attacking him because He hates him. Job is also claiming, again, that God is his adversary, which is the definition of the name Satan.

In this next tirade, Job's continues to focus on ease. *"I was at **ease**, but He has shattered me; He also has taken me by my neck, and shaken me to pieces; He has set me up for His target, His archers surround me. He pierces my heart and does not pity; He pours out my gall on the ground. He breaks me with wound upon wound; He runs at me like a warrior"* (Job 16:12-14). Job is claiming that God strangles him, uses him for an archery target, and has no pity. Job's own words reveal just how far deception has led him away from the truth of God's good character. We must all diligently resist lies that undermine the goodness of God. If we embrace these lies, the strongholds they build in our hearts will resist God Himself!

Why do Job's accusations turn to demands?

Job's attitude has deteriorated from patient endurance, to frustration, to verbal accusation. In chapter 16, Job begins to seek resolution which, in Job's mind, means that God must justify His actions. *"Oh, that one might plead for a man with God, as a man pleads for his neighbor!"* (Job 16:21). Job is getting ready to plead his case with God. Because Job is seeking justice based on his actions, the book of Job is very legal in its structure. Job allows no other explanation than blaming God, therefore his next mental leap seems logical. *"Know then that <u>God has wronged me</u>, and has surrounded me with His net"* (Job 19:6). You read correctly, Job just said God was wrong! If God is wrong, then who must be right? Job is claiming that he is smarter than God! Since pride does go before a fall (Proverbs 16:18), Job is about to be humbled.

Why are we aware of an island of truth in Job's sea of confusion?

Job continues to accuse God in chapter 19:10-11,22: *"He breaks me down on every side, And I am gone; my hope He has uprooted like a tree. He has also kindled His wrath against me, And He counts me as one of His enemies. Why do you persecute me as God does, and are not satisfied with my flesh?"* After these unfounded accusations we have some of the most quoted verses from Job, *"<u>For I know that my Redeemer lives, and He shall stand at last on the earth; and after my skin is destroyed, this I know, that in my flesh I shall see God</u>"* (Job 19:25-26). Many of you may know these verses. In fact, they may be the only verses that you know from the book of Job other than Job 1:21, *"...Naked I came from my mother's womb, And naked shall I *return there. The LORD gave, and the LORD has taken away; Blessed be the name of the LORD."*

Although Job 19:25-26 are beautiful verses of truth, are they a typical representation of what Job has been saying? No, they are not. The reason you may know them is that they are some of the only positive faith-filled words that Job speaks. They are, figuratively speaking, like an island of truth in the sea of Job's confusion. What are the odds of you, the reader, being familiar with these few positive words that Job speaks? Most of you were probably unaware of the outlandish statements that make up the bulk of Job's comments. Given the length of the book of Job, the odds that you would only know these few verses are staggering. Why would many of us know Job's few positive comments and not know the overabundance of his negative statements? The one word answer is deception!

Deception, under the guise of religion, will take a small part of the full counsel of God and use that small piece of truth to manipulate our understanding. This practice is wicked. We must take the whole counsel of God. To pick and choose is demonic. A works-focused religion has seduced many church leaders to teach from these two verses while they are surrounded by practically an ocean of Job's outlandish comments. This picking and choosing is a deceptive manipulation of God's word. The evil intention behind this is to destroy our hope.

The selective choosing of these positive verses can result in the following progression of thinking, "Job endured such difficult affliction then I guess there is nothing I can do if it happens to me." Or, "If Job's understanding was as awesome as these verses insinuate, then we should also embrace his understanding that God does bad things to us." **These verses are used to support the erroneous conclusion that Job fully understood God.** If someone with a works-focused mindset teaches from Job, they usually concentrate on two areas. The first being God's commendation of Job (Job 1:8) and the second being Job's reference to his Redeemer (Job 19:25-26) which we have been discussing. We seldom hear teaching about the vast majority of Job's other statements. This selective teaching is an effective demonic strategy to manipulate the truth.

Why does Job vacillate on the wicked being punished?

Job changes his mind throughout the book on whether he believes the wicked are punished in this life. One minute he is adamant that they are and the next minute he is confident that they are not. His timing in voicing these passionate opposing opinions is very revealing about where Job has placed his confidence. In Job 27:13-17 he passionately talks about how the wicked are going to be punished. *"This is the portion of a wicked man with God, And the heritage of oppressors, received from the Almighty: If his children are multiplied, it is for the sword; And his offspring shall not be satisfied with bread. Those who survive him shall be buried in death, And their widows shall not weep, Though he heaps up silver like dust, And piles up clothing like clay — He may pile it up, but the just will wear it, And the innocent will divide the silver."*

I believe Job 27:5-6 is a key to why Job is so adamant at this particular time that the wicked are punished: *"Far be it from me That I should say you are right; <u>Till I die I will not put away my integrity from me. My righteousness I hold fast, and will not let it go</u>; My heart shall not reproach me as long as I live."* Job had just finished strengthening himself in his own righteousness, therefore he passionately believed the wicked had to be punished. In other words, since **I** am righteous **I** should not be punished, but the wicked will have to be punished because they are not righteous like **me**.

Job's Confessions of Confusion

If we try coming to God based on our own performance, then our world will always revolve around us!

Earlier Job, just as passionately, proclaims that the wicked are not punished: *"Why do the wicked live and become old, Yes, become mighty in power? Their descendants are established with them in their sight, And their offspring before their eyes. Their houses are safe from fear, neither is the rod of God upon them. Their bull breeds without failure; their cow calves without miscarriage. They send forth their little ones like a flock, and their children dance. They sing to the tambourine and harp, And rejoice to the sound of the flute. They spend their days in wealth, And in a moment go down to the grave"* (Job 21:7-13). At this moment, Job's tragedy has him questioning his righteous works which have been his foundation. With his works foundation now unstable, he presumes that the guilty will get away with it. In other words, if God is not being fair with <u>me</u>, He is not fair at all. If we try coming to God based on our own performance, then our world will always revolve around us!

Lest we judge Job too harshly, strengthening ourselves in our own righteousness is a very common practice among Christians. If we see someone who is wealthy, but not following God, we may feel the need to recite how great our commitment is to Christ even though we don't have the possessions they have. This is a form of self-protection against becoming envious of their stuff. We feel the need to strengthen ourselves in what our great commitment to God has cost us so we can think: "They may be doing great now, but they will get what is coming to them." If we were truly resting in our relationship with God apart from our own works then we would not feel the need to compare. It is up to us to choose to rest in God's love irrespective of our performance. Only when we are basing our relationship with God on our performance will we feel the need to use comparison as a defense. <u>Job's vacillation on this issue is conclusive proof of how much his life was based on his own performance</u>.

Job's three friends have long discourses on how the wicked are punished: Eliphaz, 15:20-35; Bildad, 8:11-18; and Zophar, 20:4-29. They all seem to have the same understanding as Job: bad events are punishment from God. These three friends firmly agree that the wicked are punished. Notice that their firm position on this subject comes while they are in a place of personal ease. I believe they, like Job, would begin to vacillate if the foundation of their works based righteousness had been shaken.

What is the foundation for Job's defense?

The longer you study the book of Job, the more it mirrors a legal case. True to legal precedent, Job makes his summation in chapters 29-31. Before his summation Job makes a pronouncement that He believes is from the Lord. I said earlier that I believe this to be Job's statement of faith, *"And to man He said, 'Behold, the fear of the Lord, that is wisdom, and to depart from evil is understanding'"* (Job 28:28). Remember, as compared to Proverbs 9:10, this statement is woefully incorrect. It does not include God's desire for Job to know Him in relationship. Once this statement is made, Job's summary defense will be an attempt to prove that he has adhered to this statement of faith.

For three chapters Job pleads his own righteousness. Here is a sample: *"Because **I** delivered the poor who cried out, the fatherless and the one who had no helper. The blessing of a perishing man came upon me, and **I** caused the widow's heart to sing for joy. **I** put on righteousness, and it clothed me; **my** justice was like a robe and a turban. **I** was eyes to the blind, and **I** was feet to the lame. **I** was a father to the poor, and **I** searched out the case that*

I did not know. I broke the fangs of the wicked, and plucked the victim from his teeth" (Job 29:12-17 emphasis added).

Notice, the focus of Job's attention was on his actions. After Job finishes his final summary, He then indirectly asks God to show up, *"Oh, that I had one to hear me! Here is my mark. Oh, that the Almighty would answer me, that my Prosecutor (accuser) had written a book!"* (Job 31:35 emphasis added). Due to his perception of being wronged by God, Job has developed an attitude which exposes his underlying religious pride. Speaking of the above book which he wishes his accuser (God) would write, Job's says, *"Surely I would carry it on my shoulder, And bind it on me like a crown; I would declare to Him the number of my steps; Like a prince I would approach Him"* (Job 31:36-37). Job's terror of God is definitely gone and what remains is his arrogant self-righteous pride. Since Job has chosen to make his legal defense based upon his actions then, per his request, the Judge of all the earth is about to try his case.

Why did Job lose his incentive for serving God?

Job's service for God was based out of the fear (dread) that he had of Him. Job's duties were performed in order to pacify God. Someone with a works-focused religion believes they are pacifying God through their actions. However, when those actions no longer achieve the desired results, there no longer remains a motivation to serve God. What if we are giving our time and money to God's work and still do not have enough to cover our expenses? Or, what if we are going to church regularly and life is still difficult? Then, why keep doing it? In our reasoning, God should be helping us because He can see everything we are doing. If He is not going to help us, then we no longer have any incentive to serve Him?

We can place strings on our relationship with God. We can create our own contract with God which says, "If I do this, then You should do that." These contracts are selfish attempts to use our own works to manipulate God for our benefit. Our self-centered works can never be used in an attempt to bargain with God because they are so far below the unselfish work of Jesus. God's covenant is founded on the better foundation of Christ's self-sacrificing work, not on our own self-centered attempts at righteousness.

The following scripture conveys a message about how to walk in this life no matter what happens. *"Though the fig tree may not blossom, Nor fruit be on the vines; Though the labor of the olive may fail, And the fields yield no food; Though the flock may be cut off from the fold, And there be no herd in the stalls —Yet I will rejoice in the LORD, I will joy in the God of my salvation. The LORD God is my strength; He will make my feet like deer's feet, And He will make me walk on my high hills"* (Habakkuk 3:17-19). Notice, this passage is centered on relationship with God, not the circumstances around us. It is easy to distinguish this passage from some of the things Job has been saying. Job has constantly been defending his integrity, and speaking about his own works. Job did not rejoice or find joy in his God. I don't believe Job knew that this was even possible. Habakkuk is telling us how to strengthen ourselves in God and not in our circumstances. Job was standing on the wrong foundation, but things are about to change.

CHAPTER 11

EXPLAINING CONTROVERSIAL PASSAGES IN JOB PART 1

How do we address the apparent contradictions in Job?

In this chapter we will begin to address, individually, the apparent contradictions that occur in the book of Job. We may be confronted by someone who might use these seemingly conflicting statements in an attempt to defend their personal understanding of God. This is usually due to their misunderstanding of sovereignty which leads them to the mistaken belief that God can do both good and evil. It is important to be aware of these apparent contradictions in order to lead someone out of their misconceptions about God's character. However, it is even more important that we understand them to strengthen our own personal understanding of the goodness of God.

As we understand God's true nature more fully, the explanations of these apparent discrepancies will no longer be just mental arguments; they will become heart-felt convictions! Through God's wisdom our initial focus has been on Job's relationship with God. By first understanding Job's relationship with God, we have gained invaluable insight that will help us discern the hidden clues to these difficult passages. Understanding Job's mindset gives us insight into our own motivations for security and rest. It is important for us to understand how these desires can influence our relationship with God. Now we can study God's word through relationship, not just through theology. Correct doctrine comes through relationship, not through mental analysis.

What about God's declaration that Job is right?

Job 1:21 declares that the Lord gives and takes away. I have made it very clear that this is an incorrect understanding that Job is embracing which clearly exposes his misunderstanding about the character of God. However, the next verse says, *"In all this Job did not sin nor charge God with wrong"* (Job 1:22). If Job is as deceived as I claim him to be, then how could this verse be true? The answer is very simple. In Job's mind, God is acting just like Job thinks He should act, therefore Job does not blame God for what has happened to him. It is not a sin to be confused. Job is neither sinning nor judging God's action as wrong. Job clearly believes that God did cause these horrible tragedies which included the death of his own children. If we were judged for being wrong, we would all be in a hopeless situation.

We do not actually enter into judgment until we judge the motives of why someone did what they did.

I would like to explain what it means "to judge." If I were to say that several students were late for my class that would be an observation. If I were to say that those same students were late for class because they did not value my teaching, that would be judging or assigning blame. We do not actually enter into judgment until we judge the motives of why someone did what they did. Job is not judging God's motives and therefore, he is not in sin. We must all remember, while it is safe to be an observer, it is dangerous to judge someone's motives which only God can truly know.

Explaining Controversial Passages in Job—Part 1

No one has a right to demean Job's character because, according to God, Job's character is incontestable. God said that Job is blameless, upright, and there is no one like him on the earth. To question Job's character is to be in disagreement with God Himself. <u>Like many of us who try to follow God with a pure heart, Job's character is not the problem; the problem is his understanding</u>. Job is one of the most dedicated men you will ever read about, but he is also one of the most deceived on the subject of God's character. It is important that we have compassion on those who have been trapped in Satan's lies regarding earning their heavenly Father's approval. It is only natural that people who strive to have a relationship with God based on their works will feel the need to defend Job's character.

What about the hedge around Job?

Satan makes this accusation about Job and what God has done for him in Job 1:9-10, *"So Satan answered the Lord and said, 'Does Job fear God for nothing? <u>Have You not made a hedge</u> around him, around his household, and around all that he has on every side? You have blessed the work of his hands, and his possessions have increased in the land."* Satan is claiming that Job only serves God for His protection and blessing. Given Job's fears, there may be some truth in that statement, but what about Satan's claim that God has a hedge of protection around Job?

The name <u>Satan</u> means the adversary. Adversaries bring accusations. Notice that Satan disputes Job's motives. This seems to be his standard operating procedure. The first recorded accusation was to accuse God of impure motives (Genesis 3), and Satan seldom changes his tactics. The tough question still remains: did God have a hedge around Job, and more importantly, did

God remove it? If not, then how was Satan able to destroy Job's possessions and annihilate his family?

I have heard an explanation which says that Satan was unaware of the authority that he possessed over mankind at this time. I do not believe this to be true because of what John 10:10a reveals about Satan's nature, *"The thief does not come except to steal, and to kill, and to destroy..."* Satan's agenda is the destruction of mankind. Any newly acquired knowledge of his authority would have meant the destruction of the human race. There is no historical proof of this happening. I would, however, like to narrow the focus of this theory of Satan being unaware of his authority because I do believe it has some validity in the individual life of Job.

Job's fears of impending destruction have brought him into agreement with Satan's agenda.

I do not agree with the idea that Satan had no knowledge of his ability to cause destruction. I believe the issue is that Satan has no ability to comprehend faith. Remember, faith supersedes the time period in which we live and is also more powerful than any natural law. Faith and trust must be thought of as two sides of the same coin. You cannot have faith in God without having trust in your relationship with Him (Hebrews 11:6). To have faith you must not only believe God exists, but you must trust in His goodness. I do not believe Satan can fully understand the concept of faith which is trusting in God.

My point is that Satan cannot know how much the motives of Job's heart are based on trusting God. He can see Job's religious works, but he is unable to know how much of Job's faith falls short of genuine relationship. Satan is unaware of how much Job's protection depends on his agreement with God. Since, no relationship with God is stagnant, I believe Job's incorrect view of God has caused a deterioration in their relationship. Satan would have been unable to see this deterioration, so he does have more access to Job than he realizes. <u>I believe this is not caused from a hedge that God is taking down, but from unbelief that is growing in Job's heart</u>. Think of it as Job's shield of faith which, I believe, is becoming weaker and weaker.

Job's increased fixation on his fear had opened an ever-widening door of vulnerability. Job's fears of impending destruction have brought him into agreement with Satan's agenda. His agreement with fear removed the hedge of protection; not God. This is the opposite of James 4:7, *"Therefore submit to God. Resist the devil and he will flee from you."* Job had unknowingly embraced a spirit of fear which had stripped him of his power, deceived him about God's love, and confused his mind. *"For God has not given us a spirit of fear, but of power and of love and of a sound mind"* (2 Timothy 1:7). This verse makes it absolutely clear that this fear is not from God.

Is Job trusting in his performance?

Job has been trying to achieve rest in his life by attempting to pacify God through his works. This is very similar to a religious form of penance: works done to pay God off for our sins. In Islam, you need to say your prayers five times a day kneeling toward Mecca. Is this relational? Maybe for some Muslims it is, but if they are doing it to appease Allah so that he will not be angry with them or kill them, that is not at all relational. This means that, at this point in his life, Job is a perfect representation of a religious person. Many people believe Christianity is just another religion, but it is not. Christianity is not a religion; it is a relationship with God, provided by Christ. Job seems to be unaware of his ability to have a relationship with God.

Think about all the interesting questions that Job might have asked if he had met someone like Abraham who had an active relationship with God. He would have been astounded that God had been communicating with Abraham personally. Job could have asked, "He told you to move that far away? He actually came and ate with you? What was He like? So, He didn't want to destroy Sodom, really? You had a son at 101, just because He promised? He saved your son at the last second?" I believe Job would have been excited to learn from Abraham that God was so much more relational than he believed Him to be.

The only way to make it through difficult circumstances, without becoming angry at God, is to actually know Him.

What happens when the desire of our heart is for life to go along without difficulties and, at the same time, we do not trust God? If you think about this question for a moment you will realize that this is the exact scenario in which most people find themselves. With this mindset, when things go badly in our lives, it is inevitable that we will turn against God. The only way to make it through difficult circumstances, without becoming angry at God, is to actually know Him. <u>No one blames someone they are sure loves them</u>.

God has been rewarding Job with material possessions and children. However, God wanted to give Job the bigger spiritual reward spoken of in Proverbs 9:10b, *"And the knowledge of the Holy One is understanding."* God wants to give Job more of Himself. Job is receiving rewards that perish such as camels and sheep, but the true reward is what Abraham received, to be called a friend of God. Or, like the reward of David, to be called a man after God's own heart. True lasting rewards are based on a relationship with God. This is what Job does not have. God wants to have this kind of relationship with Job, but because Job's heart has been deceived, God is unable to reward Job with the peace and rest that a closeness to Him would provide.

Was Job right about adversity coming from God?

Job said we should accept adversity from God, but then the Bible says Job did not sin with his lips concerning this. How is this possible? *"Then his wife said to him, 'Do you still hold fast to your integrity? Curse God and die!' But he said to her, 'You speak as one of the foolish women speaks. Shall we indeed accept good from God, and shall we not accept adversity?'* <u>*In all this Job did not sin with his lips*</u>" (Job 2:9-10). The answer to this apparent conflict is the same answer I gave regarding the issue of Job saying God gives and takes away.

When your image of God does not fit the true character of God, you have actually created an idol.

Job is simply stating what he believes his version of God would do: give good as well as adversity. Job's statement, though completely false, is still not a sin. It is not a sin to be wrong. For example, when Jesus appeared to Saul on the road to Damascus He did not judge him for his persecution of Christians done in ignorance (Acts 9:1-6). Job is actually very tolerant of how he believes his version of God is acting. Remember, his fortitude in the face of difficulty is what makes Job so admired by those who have a similar commitment theology.

When your image of God does not fit the true character of God, you have actually created an idol. Job does not worship the reality of Who God is, but a false image of a God that he has created from his own understanding. We must resist bowing down to a version of God that we have personally created. The danger is that we will always get angry when our "idol" acts differently than we expect him to act. We are not supposed to change God to conform to our image, but we are to be conformed to His image. God does not need to change, we do. *"For whom He foreknew, He also predestined <u>to be conformed to the image of His Son</u>, that He might be the firstborn among many brethren"* (Romans 8:29).

Did God send fire down from heaven?

In Job 1:16 we read about fire from God, *"While he was still speaking, <u>another</u> also came and said, "<u>The fire of God fell from heaven</u> and burned up the sheep and the servants, and consumed them; and I alone have escaped to tell you!"* First of all, who is saying this? It is another servant of Job's. It appears that, like Job, this servant is predisposed to believe that tragedy comes from God. Using the words of God in the book of Job along with other scriptural evidence we can prove beyond any doubt that this fire did not come from God as this servant reported. In Job 1:12, it is clear who will be acting against Job, *"And the LORD said to Satan, 'Behold, all that he has <u>is in your power</u>; only do not lay a hand on his person.' So <u>Satan</u> went out from the presence of the LORD."* **The Lord is not bringing any tragedy on Job, Satan is.**

The next pertinent question is this: does Satan have power to bring fire down from Heaven? In Revelation 13:13 we read where the anti-Christ, operating on Satan's behalf, does have that power, *"He performs great signs, so that <u>he even makes fire come down from heaven</u> on the earth <u>in the sight of men</u>."* I am not claiming that Satan always has this power, but it is definitely mentioned here. We must also look closely at another example of fire from heaven that was seen in Elijah's ministry.

Explaining Controversial Passages in Job—Part 1

In 2 Kings 1:10 Elijah calls fire down from heaven, *"So Elijah answered and said to the captain of fifty, 'If I am a man of God, then let fire come down from heaven and consume you and your fifty men.' And fire came down from heaven and consumed him and his fifty."* Jesus had an understanding of these scriptures which was completely different from that of His disciples. He makes it clear that their desire to repeat Elijah's feat is coming from another spirit, not the Spirit of God.

When Jesus's disciples were offended by a group of Samaritans this was their reaction, *"And when His disciples James and John saw this, they said, 'Lord, do You want us to command fire to come down from heaven and consume them, just as Elijah did?' But He turned and rebuked them, and said, 'You do not know what manner of spirit you are of. For the Son of Man did not come to destroy men's lives but to save them...'"* (Luke 9:54-55). God's desire is never to destroy life, but to save life. Elijah, driven by personal offense, had let his righteous anger turn into fleshly wrath which we are warned against doing. *"So then, my beloved brethren, let every man be swift to hear, slow to speak, slow to wrath; for the wrath of man does not produce the righteousness of God"* (James 1:19-20). <u>The fire that Elijah called down from heaven did not come from God or Jesus</u> could not have warned His disciples against repeating it.

Retribution is God's business, not ours.

We have been given more authority than we realize. We should never curse anyone, and we should be careful what we say in judgment of others. Our authority is activated when we believe it by faith. Elijah believed in his authority, yet his authority was able to be misused for evil. We must learn from Jesus's humble example how to overlook an offense. Jesus rebuked his disciples for even considering personal retribution. We should let our words be kind, even using them to bless our enemies. Retribution is God's business, not ours. *"Beloved, do not avenge yourselves, but rather give place to wrath; for it is written, 'Vengeance is Mine, I will repay' says the Lord. Therefore 'If your enemy is hungry, feed him; if he is thirsty, give him a drink; for in so doing you will heap coals of fire on his head.'* <u>*Do not be overcome by evil*</u>*, but overcome evil with good"* (Romans 12:19-21).

Elijah had turned his anger against the wrong enemy by being overcome by evil. *"For we do not wrestle against flesh and blood, but against principalities, against powers, against the rulers of the darkness of this age, against spiritual hosts of wickedness in the heavenly places"* (Ephesian 6:12). Elijah's anger had killed men, but had done nothing to destroy the evil behind their wicked leader. It is very important that we realize that people are **never** our enemy, only the evil forces behind them.

Did the wind that killed Job's children come from God?

The last and worst of all tragedies to come upon Job in chapter one was the death of all his children. *"While he was still speaking, another also came and said, 'Your sons and daughters were eating and drinking wine in their oldest brother's house, and suddenly a great wind came from across the wilderness and struck the four corners of the house, and it fell on the young people, and they are dead; and I alone have escaped to tell you!'"* (Job 1:18-19). Was this wind sent from God? According to God's Own words in Job 1:12, the wind must be attributed to Satan. But, that raises another question: Who can influence the laws of nature? Do we have the evidence that someone other than God can influence nature? Yes, we do.

"And a great windstorm arose, and the waves beat into the boat, so that it was already filling. But He (Jesus) was in the stern, asleep on a pillow. And they awoke Him and said to Him, 'Teacher, do You not care that we are perishing?' Then <u>He arose and rebuked the wind</u>, and said to the sea, 'Peace, be still!' And the wind ceased and there was a great calm" (Mark 4:37-39). This storm could not have been sent by God, because Jesus rebuked it. Jesus had made it clear that He only did what His Father instructed Him to do. *"…Most assuredly, I say to you, the Son can do nothing of Himself, but what He sees the Father do; for whatever He does, the Son also does in like manner"* (John 5:19). God could not have caused this storm because Jesus's stopping it would have violated His teaching on the laws of the kingdom, *"Every kingdom divided against itself is brought to desolation, and a house divided against a house falls."* (Luke 11:17). One thing we can be certain of is that this storm was not from God.

This storm could have been just a typical storm like those that were common on the Sea of Galilee. However, I believe this particular storm was influenced by Satan for a very strategic purpose. As the events are recorded in Mark, chapter 5, we know there is a demon possessed man on the other side of the sea. Satan knows that Jesus has the power to deliver him, therefore he does not want to lose control over this person he has possessed for so long. Keeping Jesus away will remove the possibility that He will set this demon possessed man free. His plan failed and, not only was the man set free, he became a missionary in the very area where he was formerly known as being demon possessed. His redeemed life was a powerful living testimony as everyone could visibly see the miracle that Jesus had performed in his life.

So, the question remains: who can influence the weather? The biblical answer is a little hard to believe: it is simply whoever has the faith for it. Here are a few biblical examples: *"Elijah was a man with a nature like ours, and <u>he prayed earnestly that it would not rain</u>; <u>and it did not rain</u> on the land for three years and six months. And<u> he prayed again</u>, <u>and the heaven gave rain</u>, and the earth produced its fruit"* (James 5:17-18). Supernatural acts which override the laws of nature are possible through our faith. *"And he (Jesus) said, 'Come'. And when Peter was come down out of the ship, he walked on the water, to go to Jesus. But when he (Peter) saw the wind boisterous, <u>he was afraid; and beginning to sink</u>, he cried, saying, 'Lord, save me'"* (Matthew 14:29-30). If Peter's fear caused him to sink then it was his belief in the word of Jesus that caused him to be able to walk on water which defied natural law.

I know these things do not happen often, but the Bible gives us accounts of amazing events that have happen when someone believed. The next example is the most amazing of all, *"Then Joshua spoke to the LORD in the day when the LORD delivered up the Amorites before the children of Israel, and he said in the sight of Israel: '<u>Sun, stand still</u> over Gibeon; And Moon, in the Valley of Aijalon.' <u>So the sun stood still</u>, <u>And the moon stopped</u>, Till the people had revenge Upon their enemies. Is this not written in the Book of Jasher? <u>So the sun stood still in the midst of heaven, and did not hasten to go down for about a whole day</u>. And there has been no day like that, before it or after it, <u>that the LORD heeded the voice of a man</u>; for the LORD fought for Israel"* (Joshua 10:12-14). The opinion that **only** God could have caused the wind which led to the death of Job's children, does not have a scriptural foundation. It is developed through a false understanding of God's Sovereignty, and it is not biblically accurate.

Explaining Controversial Passages in Job—Part 1

How will works-focused religion fail?

Earlier we saw that Job's only hope was in life after death. However, Job is accused of having hope in something else. *"Is not your reverence your confidence? And the integrity of your ways your hope?"* (Job 4:6). I think this exposes a progression in Job's heart that takes place as these tragedies unfold. I think Job was originally hoping that his own works would protect him from trouble. But, once it is clear that his works have not protected him, then Job loses all hope in this present life. Job's hope had been built on the extremely weak foundation of his own works. The only strong foundation is the love of God, which Job has yet to comprehend.

I believe in the days in which we live there will be a collapse in the religious structures which have been built by trusting in the works of men. As the idols of men's religious works fall, they will bow before the soon returning Christ. As Christians, I believe we are about to understand relationship with God and our brothers and sisters in Christ like never before. In our renewed understanding, we will go out and demonstrate relationship with God and not a dead religious system of do's and don'ts. I believe those who have truly made Jesus their Lord will begin to genuinely know God. This will no longer be only head knowledge, it will be heart knowledge as well. I believe this will be in fulfillment of the prophecy recorded in Daniel 11:32, *"…but the people <u>who know their God</u> shall be strong, and carry out great exploits."*

The false idols of religion will become more and more evident as they are exposed in the light of those who have true relationship with God. These exalted idols of religion will be some of the last things to fall before Christ's return. Satan has been manipulating the hearts of men and women through their own religious works, but his manipulation is about to be revealed. In the void of the fallen idols of religion, God is about to raise up the standard of His love and relationship with us. As Isaiah 21:9b states, *"Babylon is fallen, is fallen! And all the carved images of her gods He has broken to the ground."* I believe Paul's prayer in Ephesians 3:19 is about to be fulfilled in the hearts of many believers, *"to know the love of Christ which passes knowledge; that you may be filled with all the fullness of God."*

CHAPTER 12

JOB MEETS GOD

Why did Job's quest for answers not work?

The bulk of the middle of the book of Job is about Job and his friends looking for answers without spiritual understanding. It has been clearly established that Job's three friends were true friends, but their ability to find answers was limited by their lack of knowledge of God. Understanding the book of Job is so critical for believers because it is a book about a man and his friends who, while already believers, still <u>do not know their</u> <u>God</u>. Today, that is a position many believers find themselves in due to Satan's deceptive tactics against the church. We must truly know God to have accurate understanding. *"The fear of the LORD is the beginning of wisdom, And <u>the knowledge of the Holy One</u> <u>is understanding</u>"* (Proverbs 9:10). Many of us have the first part of this verse down; but, like Job and his friends, we are severely lacking in the "knowledge of the Holy One".

> ***Job's quest for answers did not work because he was looking for answers outside of his relationship with God.***

Our desire to have answers can be so strong that we forget to pursue the One who has the answers. *"And you will seek Me and find Me, when you search for Me with all your heart. I will be found by you, says the LORD"* (Jeremiah 29:13-14a). In the knowledge of God Himself is where all of our questions will be answered. Our passion to make sense of our fallen world apart from knowing God will only leave us with bitter disillusionment or arrogant misunderstandings of the truth. <u>God never commands</u>

us to look for answers, but He often asks us to look for Him. Job's quest for answers did not work because he was looking for answers outside of his relationship with God.

I have not yet covered the comments made by Job's three friends: Eliphaz, Bildad, and Zophar. These friends, while compassionate in the beginning, became increasingly frustrated with Job. Their frustration was born from Job's refusal to admit any guilt. Their paradigm was so narrow that they believed bad events could only happen as punishment from God upon the guilty. Job's refusal to admit guilt, while he was still receiving what they perceived to be God's punishment, did not fit within their understanding. Like Job, his friends have no concept of an enemy that would do them harm. Nor do they believe that something bad could happen to someone who does not deserve it. For their view of the world to work, every action must have a reciprocating response. That view could only work in a perfect world, not the one in which we all find ourselves.

Is Elihu a mediator?

Elihu is a younger man who has been listening to the conversations between Job and his three friends. He has become very angry at all four of these older men, but we do not hear him speak until chapter 32. *"Now because they were years older than he, Elihu had waited to speak to Job. When Elihu saw that there was no answer in the mouth of these three men, his wrath was aroused. So Elihu, the son of Barachel the Buzite, answered and said: "I am young in years, and you are very old; Therefore I was afraid, And dared not declare my opinion to you"* (Job 32:4-6). As we read earlier, God refutes the statements of Job's three friends, but He never refutes Elihu's words even though he is sometimes very self-aggrandizing.

Job Meets God

Here are a few comments from Elihu. *"My words come from my upright heart; my lips utter pure knowledge"* (Job 33:3). *"For truly my words are not false; one who is perfect in knowledge is with you"* (Job 36:4). Why is Elihu not corrected by God for these apparently arrogant statements? I think it is because he has been sent by God to be a mediator between Job and Himself. God sent someone to soften the stubborn ground of Job's heart hoping for repentance before He would be forced to bring correction. It is the heart of any good parent for the child to realize their error before correction is needed.

Even though Elihu makes these bold statements about himself, he takes a position of humility with Job pointing out that he is only a man and Job will not have to be afraid of him, *"Truly I am as your spokesman before God; I also have been formed out of clay. Surely no fear of me will terrify you, Nor will my hand be heavy on you"* (Job 33:6-7). Job wanted to speak with God or have a mediator, but did not believe this to be possible, *"For He is not a man, as I am, That I may answer Him, And that we should go to court together. Nor is there any mediator between us, Who may lay his hand on us both"* (Job 9:32-33). Right before Elihu appears Job cries out these words in desperation, *"Oh, that I had one to hear me!"* (Job 31:35a).

I believe Elihu is the answer to Job's prayer. I believe God is attempting to convince Job that his grievances against Him are unjust. God is doing all He can to <u>avoid</u> bringing a legal judgment against Job. God always desires mercy, not judgment. *"Who is a God like You, Pardoning iniquity And passing over the transgression of the remnant of His heritage? He does not retain His anger forever, <u>Because He delights in mercy</u>"* (Micah 7:18). Because Job is performance based in his thinking, he is desiring justice, but we can never desire justice based on our own works. *"See now, I have prepared my case, I know that I* *shall be vindicated"* (Job 13:18). Job's defense is based solely upon his own self-righteous works. That is not a position that he will be able to defend. The only viable defense must be based upon the goodness of God and His mercy. Job is oblivious to the impossibility of winning with his current defense.

Elihu can be seen as a representation of Jesus Christ. He appears to be present during most of the events in the story. His words were not refuted, and many of his statements were repeated by God Himself. Even though Elihu tries reasoning with Job, Job still refuses to relent from his works-based defense. This mirrors Christ's difficulty with the religious leaders of His day who were righteous in their own eyes. Jesus often had confrontational arguments with these men to persuade them to abandon their self-righteousness.

Do Elihu and God agree on Job's problem?

Job's problems have been magnified by his lack of understanding. Both Elihu and God concur with this assessment when they arrive on the scene. Elihu says, *"Therefore Job opens his mouth in vain; He multiplies words without knowledge"* (Job 35:16). The first words that Job ever hears from God are, *"Who is this who darkens counsel By words without knowledge?"* (Job 38:2). **For anyone to teach the book of Job from the position that Job had accurate understanding is to teach against the word of God Himself.** They have mistakenly been deceived by a religious spirit. If they truly wish to honor Job then they will take the path of humility that he took once he realized his mistake, *"You asked, 'Who is this who hides counsel without knowledge?' Therefore I have uttered what I did not understand, Things too wonderful for me, which I did not know"* (Job 42:3).

Job Meets God

God honors those who are true to their core beliefs. This is called integrity. Job, for the most part, held true to his beliefs even though those beliefs were wrong. God respects Job's integrity even though it was misguided. Jesus tells a parable in Luke 16:1-13 about a master, representing God, who commends His unjust steward because he has acted shrewdly. This servant had acted according to his beliefs, even though those beliefs were not based on trusting God. God loves Job but, like most of us, his understanding is incomplete. God can direct a moving ship; not one that is in port. God loves that Job is trying even though he doesn't know what he is really seeking. Job's heart desired rest which he believed was achievable through his works. However, God showed him that rest could not be found by anything in this world; it could only be found by trusting Him.

Why does Elihu proclaim God's Majesty?

Part of Elihu's approach to address Job's misunderstanding is to proclaim God's majesty. Why has Elihu chosen to use this approach? It is because, during his tragedy, Job's focus on his own righteousness has diminished God's greatness. The reason Job's friends have stopped speaking to him is clearly stated in Job 32:1, *"So these three men ceased to answer Job, <u>because he was righteous in his own eyes</u>."* Job had become so self-absorbed he had lost sight of the bigger picture. Self-pity is a temptation we all must fight against. Any personal difficulty will become magnified in our own eyes as we focus upon it. We must consciously resist this temptation by taking these thoughts captive (2 Corinthians 10:5).

Worship gives us the true perspective of God's greatness that we desperately need when struggling to maintain our hope.

Job could have made it through those tragedies without becoming fixated upon them if he had known how much God loved him. The most effective way for us to take thoughts captive is to replace them with thoughts of God's love. Magnifying God through worship is a way to replace these thoughts during challenging times. Worship gives us the true perspective of God's greatness that we desperately need when struggling to maintain our hope. Worship reminds us how big our God is compared to our problem. Job's belief that God has caused his troubles would have inhibited his ability to worship Him. This inhibited desire to worship caused a downward spiral as Job became even more fixated on his problems instead of God Who was his solution.

David seemed to understand the importance of worship more than anyone, *"I will call upon the Lord, who is worthy to be praised; So shall I be saved from my enemies. The pangs of death surrounded me, And the floods of ungodliness made me afraid. The sorrows of Sheol surrounded me; The snares of death confronted me. In my distress I called upon the Lord, And cried out to my God; He heard my voice from His temple, And my cry came before Him, even to His ears"* (Psalms 18:3-6). Notice how closely David linked worship to personal deliverance!

A righteousness based on works is always self-focused and not God focused; therefore, it has no power whatsoever <u>to deliver</u> anyone from trouble.

Both Elihu and God use the proclamation of God's majesty to shake Job out of his self-centeredness. Elihu: *"Remember to magnify His work, of which men have sung. Everyone has seen it; Man looks on it from afar. Behold, God is great, and we do not know Him; nor can the number of His years be discovered"* (Job 36:24-26). *"Where were you when I [God] laid the foundations of the earth?"* (Job 38:4a). Again we see that Elihu and God are on the same page in their attempt to correct Job's misunderstanding. A righteousness based on works is always self-focused and not God focused. Therefore, it has no power whatsoever <u>to deliver</u> anyone from trouble. Job's focus is himself; not the Deliverer Who can save him. It is important for all of us to learn to keep our focus on God during difficult times, while not focusing on the problem.

Is God angry with Job?

When God answers Job why does He seem to be angry? Job has slowly developed the attitude; "I guess God is wrong, because I know I'm right!" This is definitely not the smartest choice of the available options. If we ever believe an omniscient God is wrong, we are definitely deceived. Once we believe God has made a mistake and we have the correct answer, it is absolutely certain that our thinking is skewed. Somewhere we have failed to take deceptive thoughts captive, leading us to the insanity of believing that we know better than God.

God appears to Job in a whirlwind because Job imagines God as terrifying. God does not initiate fear because, *"There is no fear in love…"* (1 John 4:18). God is only highlighting Job's fear so he will realize that he is being controlled by it. A fearful perception of God will change our relationship with Him. <u>God must first break us free from our fear filled perceptions before we can receive the truth of Who He really is.</u> Another good example of God appearing to someone in a dramatic fashion is the conversion of Saul of Tarsus on the road to Damascus. Saul was blinded by the presence of the Lord as he received revelation of Who He was. (Acts 9:1-19).

The only group of people Jesus appeared to be harsh with were the religious leaders of His day. Jesus loved these leaders, so He had to be speaking to them out of love. Jesus was not being callous as we might be; He was trying to get their attention. He was resorting to this form of tough love because their hearts had become hardened through self-justification. They had reached such a point of self-deception that it was preventing them from recognizing the truth.

If God has to "yank your chain" then be assured it is a last resort for Him.

If you ever feel God getting ugly with you, I would suggest doing a self-evaluation to see where you began to justify your actions. If God has to "yank your chain", be assured it is a last resort for Him. He has certainly tried other means, but your heart has been too hard to hear them. Humble yourself quickly and ask Him to expose the level of your deception because, whatever the problem is, it has gone on far too long. God loves Job and has been trying to speak to him, but he has been blinded by the self-justification of his own righteousness.

Was Job's foundation himself?

God reveals to us in Job 40:2 just how far Job's self-righteousness has taken him, *"Shall the one who <u>contends</u> with the Almighty correct Him? He who <u>rebukes</u> God, let him answer it."* The word <u>contend</u> means to toss, grapple, or wrangle, hold a controversy. The word <u>rebuke</u> means to be right or correct, to justify, argue, chasten, convict, correction. Job disagreed with God, but over time he took it a step further. In his self-righteous pride, Job has judged God as guilty and intends to correct Him.

Job Meets God

God shows up in a powerful way to obliterate Job's arrogance in order to deal with the real issue: Job's misunderstanding. If Job had understood how loving God is, then he would have never believed Him to be guilty of the tragedies that befell him. His anger would never have led him to judge God. Many people have resentment toward God because of this same downward spiral of misunderstanding. <u>Most people, at some level, are angry at God</u>.

When we create our own lies and believe them, we are self-deceived.

Behind our resentment toward God is the driving need for answers that will help us understand our difficult circumstances. But, what happens when we cannot find answers? The quickest solution is to make up the answers ourselves, and the easiest answer is: it's God fault. The only problem is that this is not true. We fabricated this lie in order to have someone to blame. When we make up our own truth, we become our own God. Job's foundation had become himself. He had made up his own reasons why bad things happened to him. He was so sure of his own lies, he was ready to convict God for His unjust actions. When we create our own lies and believe them, we are self-deceived. It is easy for this process to become a repeating pattern. If we are living in deception, it is much easier for us to come up with our own answers rather than wait for the truth

I believe Elihu is sent by God to point out how far Job has gone down this path of self-deception. Here are several passages in which Elihu tries to reason with Job, *"Therefore listen to me, you men of understanding: Far be it from God to do wickedness, And from the Almighty to commit iniquity"* (Job 34:10). *"Surely God will never do wickedly, nor will the Almighty pervert justice"* (Job 34:12). *"Will you condemn Him who is most just? Is* it fitting to say to a king, 'You are worthless', and to nobles, 'you are wicked'"? (Job 34:17b-18). Elihu seems to get more forceful with Job as time goes on. After failing to make a dent in Job's stubbornness, Elihu confronts Job with these words, *"Do you think this is right? Do you say, 'My righteousness is more than God's'?"* (Job 35:2).

God loves Job, but Job has fallen into the trap of making up his own answers to difficult questions. These answers are lies which he has chosen to believe. His self-deception has made him consistently wrong and blinded him to the simple humility of receiving the truth. No one is able to talk any sense into Job because the foundation of Job's world has been built on his own understanding, and that understanding is built upon lies that he firmly believes.

Why does Job change so quickly?

The legitimate cry of the human heart is for relationship, not for justice.

For all of Job's rantings about being falsely mistreated, he does not have a word to say in his defense when his behavior is questioned by God. *"Then Job answered the LORD and said: 'Behold, I am vile; What shall I answer You? I lay my hand over my mouth. Once I have spoken, but I will not answer; Yes, twice, but I will proceed no further'"* (Job 40:3-5). How could Job have gone from having such a demand for justice to total repentance so quickly? It is taken for granted that if someone gives you your day in court, you would plead your case. So, why is Job's response so uncharacteristic? I believe this is because the legitimate cry of the human heart is for relationship, not for justice.

Job Meets God

In spite of all Job's religious devotion, he has never really believed he could have a personal relationship with God. *"If I called and He answered me, I would not believe that He was listening to my voice"* (Job 9:16). This is a common belief still held by many Christians. If this seems familiar then it is a testimony to how well our enemy has deceived us about the character of God. Many believers even today do not believe God hears them. David believed God heard him, *"In my distress I called upon the Lord, And cried out to my God; <u>He heard my voice</u> from His temple, And my cry came before Him, even to His ears"* (Psalm 18:6).

God does not love what you can do for Him; He loves you.

God did not send Jesus so He could redeem a bunch of servants to get His work done. He sent Jesus so He could restore His sons and daughters back into the family. God does not love what you can do for Him; He loves you. *"I will be a Father to you, And you shall be <u>My sons and daughters</u>, Says the LORD Almighty"* (2 Corinthians 6:18). *"Behold what manner of love the Father has bestowed on us, that we should be called <u>children of God</u>!"* (1 John 3:1a).

There is something in every human heart that wants to be in relationship with their heavenly Father. Job has been deceived into believing that a relationship with his heavenly Father is not possible. Job's unbelief is broken when God shows up and starts speaking to him personally. This is why he changes his attitude so quickly. He finally got what he really needed, not what he thought he needed. Romans 2:4 says, *"Or do you despise the riches of His goodness, forbearance, and longsuffering, not knowing that <u>the goodness of God leads you to repentance</u>?"* **After Job's true need for relationship was met, he no longer seeks justice.** All his complaints now seem insignificant in the presence of God.

The fact that Job repents so quickly is an indication of how wrong he had been about God's character.

It is important to realize that a fearful God could not have changed Job's heart quickly because Job had always feared God. The truth is this: even in a whirlwind with a loud voice God could not hide His goodness and mercy. **If God had been exactly the way Job had thought he was, then Job would not have needed to repent.** Job would have been right all along about this fearful, vindictive, unpredictable God. The fact that Job repents so quickly is an indication of how wrong he had been about God's character. The most enjoyable verses in this book are the following. "<u>I have heard of You</u> by the hearing of the ear, But now <u>my eye sees You</u>. Therefore I abhor myself, And repent in dust and ashes" (Job 42:5-6). Job finally meets the God Whom he has served, but not known personally.

It is always a joy filled day when someone in works-focused religion breaks free from the lies to enter into a personal relationship with God, a relationship which has nothing at all to do with their performance. It is often easier to bring a prodigal son into relationship with God than it is to convince the committed older brother. The prodigal knows his acceptance is not based on his performance while the older brother's performance can get in his way. "So he answered and said to his father, 'Lo, these many years <u>I have been serving you</u>; <u>I never transgressed your commandment at any time</u>; and yet you never gave me a young goat that I might make merry with my friends.' And he said to him, 'Son, you are always with me, and all that I have is yours'" (Luke 15:29,31). God's love for us will never be based on our performance. **Serving God based on performance will blind us to all that is already available to us as sons.** Job had thought he was a servant; but once he met God, he realized he was a son.

CHAPTER 13

EXPLAINING CONTROVERSIAL PASSAGES IN JOB PART 2

What about Elihu's difficult statement?

Elihu's words are not refuted by God, yet he makes a somewhat puzzling statement in Job 33:19, *"Man is also chastened with pain on his bed, and with strong pain in many of his bones."* Since one of God's names is Jehovah Rapha (the Lord our healer) I do not believe God can cause pain or sickness to come upon someone or He would be in conflict with Himself. Jesus, who was the fullness of God, (Colossians 2:9) never put sickness on anyone. If Jesus had done this, God's kingdom would be a kingdom divided against itself. The only viable answer I have for that passage is this: it does not say man is chastened by God. The chastening Elihu is referring to could be the consequences of the life choices we make that result in pain and suffering.

A few verses later Elihu speaks about the graciousness of God's mediator, *"If there is a messenger for him, A mediator, one among a thousand, To show man His uprightness, <u>Then He is gracious to him</u>, and says, '<u>Deliver him</u> from going down to the Pit; I have found a ransom'"* (Job 33:23-24). These verses are more in line with the truth of God's character and reflect the overwhelming majority of Elihu's statements.

CAN I TRUST GOD

What about God's incitement against Job?

After Job's first round of tragedies the Lord again brings up Job's commendation to Satan but immediately following, God says something very unusual, *"And still he holds fast to his integrity, although <u>you incited Me against him, to destroy him without cause</u>"* (Job 2:3b). I personally believe the verse must be read as follows: And still he (Job) holds fast to his (Job's) integrity although you (Satan) incited me (God) against him (Job) so that you (Satan) could destroy him (Job) without cause. First, let's tackle the second phrase: "to destroy him without cause". This has to be referring to Satan's attack on Job because we know that God was not responsible for these attacks. But, this leaves the question: How is Satan inciting God?

The word incite in the King James Version is <u>movedst</u> which means to prick or stimulate, implying: to seduce, entice, move or persuade. So the important question is what is the basis of Satan's provocation of God? How is Satan prodding God to get Him to do something? I believe the answer is found in Job 1:9-10, *"So Satan answered the LORD and said, '<u>Does Job fear God for nothing</u>? Have You not made a hedge around him, around his household, and around all that he has on every side? You have blessed the work of his hands, and his possessions have increased in the land'."* The key here is that Satan is provoking God with partial truth.

The only way you can get a righteous judge to rule in your favor is to have at least some truth on your side. Satan does have a valid argument against Job. Job's relationship with God is predicated upon what he will get out of the relationship. Job is bartering with God, using his good works as currency, expecting to receive in return a restful and trouble free life. Satan's accusation is true because there is a selfish motive behind Job's sacrifices. God, as the righteous Judge, is pricked by this truth. God cannot be moved to act on a lie. As further proof that God is not behind the tragedies against Job, the phrase <u>without cause</u> means devoid of cost, reason, or advantage; in vain. God is saying that there is no point to this action, which is further evidence that He is not behind it. God never acts in vain.

Does God Allow Satan access to Job?

In order to answer this question we must first understand that God and Satan are not equals. God is a non-created eternal Being with no beginning and no end. Lucifer was a created angel who rebelled against God, was thrown out of heaven, and is now called Satan (the adversary). Picture in your mind a red clay brick that represents Satan. The reason this is a good representation of Satan is because, compared to God, Satan is as dumb as a brick. As far as intelligence goes, this is as close a comparison as you can have. There is the omniscient God and there is the brick.

The brick's intelligence is in no way equal with the eternal God Who created him, yet he still attempted to usurp his Creator. This brick does the same predictable things over and over again. But, this time the brick has a valid argument. The brick says, Job does not serve You for nothing. God does not want to see anything bad happen to Job because He delights in mercy (Micah 7:18b). God is jealous to have a closer relationship with Job because that is what is in Job's best interest. God has run out of options to pursue a relationship with Job. Job's own fears have opened a doorway for the predictable actions of Satan to become an avenue to accomplish the intended end. God wants to have a relationship with Job that will have no strings attached. Because of God's integrity He has been unable to achieve that relationship through the Self-imposed limits of His Own word.

This is similar to a marriage relationship in which one spouse discovers that the other spouse is only with them for what they can get out of them. This can be hurtful because we really want them to love us just for us. God exposes an opening that Satan has into Job's life. **What happened in Job's life should never happen to a born-again believer.** In Job's day, there was no revelation of God's love poured out for humanity on the cross; there was no written scripture for Job to read; and there was no indwelling Spirit of God, which we have today. God had little to work with to instruct Job in His true character, but this did not stop God's desire for relationship.

God is left with one predictable avenue to work through: the brick. God knows that Satan will do what Satan will do. God is utilizing the opening Satan already had into Job's life through Job's agreement to embrace fear. Some people may become upset with my explanation and say things like: "You mean God knew Satan would do this?" God is omniscient therefore, yes, He knew what Satan would do. God is the one Who brought up Job to Satan in the first place. To me, this indicates a set-up. It is my belief that during this time period God has exhausted all other possible options. God <u>now</u> has multiple avenues of communication. I am not saying that this is the only explanation for these events, but at this point in my life, I believe this is the only viable option.

Does Satan's accusation of Job prove to be true?

We can prove the truth of Satan's accusation quite easily. God tells us that Job feared God, but later Job claims to abandon the fear of God, *"To him who is afflicted, kindness should be shown by his friend, <u>Even though he forsakes the fear of the Almighty</u>"* (Job 6:14). If you are serving God for what you can get out of Him, what will happen to your desire to serve Him when He is no longer providing what you want? Job has been serving God for what he can get out of him: **rest**. Once that rest is no longer provided, Job was no longer motivated to serve God.

Job had initiated a one-sided contract with God. Job must have been thinking, "If I do this then God will do that." The problem is that God never agreed to Job's arrangement. We often do the very same thing. The mental contract we create might say, "Since I am going to church and giving faithfully, God will make sure that none of my children go astray." What happens to our relationship with God if one of our children gets on drugs? Our desire to serve God is diminished because we perceive that God has violated our agreement. The same thing happens if our mental contract says that as long as we serve God, He will keep sickness away from us. If we discover we have cancer, then we are angry at God for violating our agreement.

Notice all of our mental agreements are tied to our performance. God never signs off on our performance-based contracts because His love is never based on our performance. His love is unconditional. The only true covenant or contract that God has made with man originated in the heart of God, and was executed by God Himself through Jesus Christ. That contract has been executed with all its benefits already provided through faith in Jesus. That contract can never fail, but we can fail to receive its benefits through our unbelief.

> *There is simply opposition in this world and trouble comes.*

I have seen many Bible college students sacrifice a lot to pursue God's call to be trained for ministry. Whether they verbalized it or not, they may think, "Ok God, I expect you to take care of me since I gave up so much to do what you asked." But, as soon as the rent is late or the car breaks down, they begin to doubt God's instruction. This is all based on an unreasonable desire for things to go well. This is the same desire for ease and rest which Job had. But, the problem is: things do not always go well. God was not wrong to ask you to go to school, and it was not a mistake to obey. There is simply opposition in this world and trouble comes. You probably have not made a mistake and certainly God has not abandoned you. I like to use the analogy of a flat tire to explain that problems happen. Remember, in this life, there are nails in the road.

Be very careful what manner of agreement you fabricate between God and yourself. Job apparently had done this, so when his idea that God was supposed to protect him did not materialize, he believes God to be unjust. Job holds on to this fabricated contract for almost forty chapters because he is so determined to be right. However, no one can hide that kind of anger and frustration forever. <u>Self-righteous religion will never hold up in tough times because it is you standing in your own strength</u>. God cannot allow you to stand in your own strength. He will only allow you to stand in the strength of the victory won by His Son.

Is God validating the statements of Job?

This passage is one of the more difficult ones to explain, but I will share with you what I believe. "*And so it was, after the LORD had spoken these words to Job, that the LORD said to Eliphaz the Temanite, 'My wrath is aroused against you and your two friends, <u>for you have not spoken of Me what is right, as My servant Job has</u>*' (Job 42:7). As we have seen, Job said many things that were not true, especially about the character of God.

Explaining Controversial Passages in Job—Part 2

One explanation of this apparent contradiction is that God is speaking of what Job said after he met with Him. Once Job had repented, his sins were no longer remembered. *"As far as the east is from the west, So far has He removed our transgressions from us"* (Psalm 103:12). A good example of this principle would be the faith of Sarah mentioned in Hebrews, chapter 11. There is no recalling of her having laughed at God's initial pronouncement that she would have a child in her old age (Genesis 18:12).

A second explanation is that, because Job never wavered in his integrity or understanding of God, God honored his integrity even though it was devoid of knowledge. Job was not a hypocrite and he repented immediately when confronted with truth. Repentance based on revealed truth is honorable to God. Because of Job's many incorrect statements about God, I believe one or both of these to be a plausible explanation.

God is definitely not pleased with how Job's three friends have behaved. I think it is mainly because, as time went on, they didn't respond in love. In their growing impatience, they exhibited a lack of compassion by becoming Job's accusers. Their behavior is unacceptable to God. God will only accept a prayer on their behalf which is offered by Job. I believe this is God's method of repairing the damage to these relationships. His heart is for Job to embrace forgiveness toward his friends, so that Job will not harbor resentment for what they have done. An added benefit of Job's intercession is that his friends must acknowledge the full restoration of his spiritual position, even though it will take time for his wealth to be restored.

CHAPTER 14

SUMMARIZING THE POWERFUL LESSONS FROM JOB

Why do most people think like Job?

The number one reason the book of Job is so relevant today is that most people still have the same mindset Job had before he met God. Even many Christians still have the same misunderstanding about God's character as Job did. Their misunderstanding is rooted in the deception that their relationship with God is based solely upon what they do. *"Behold, the fear of the Lord, that is wisdom, and <u>to depart from evil</u> is understanding"* (Job 28:28). God does not desire a relationship with you based on what you can do for Him, He desires you. As we clearly saw, reverence for God is only the beginning; knowing Him brings us understanding. *"The fear of the LORD is the beginning of wisdom, and the knowledge of the Holy One is understanding"* (Proverbs 9:10).

A works-focused religion is centered on <u>doing</u>. This makes the foundation of religion us, not God. Fearing God and shunning evil is based upon what we are doing, not upon trusting in the goodness of God. If we are religiously doing all the right things then we expect circumstances in our life to go well. If for some reason life is not good, then we will probably blame God. After all, it can't be us, because we are <u>doing</u> everything right. "Well, I guess God must give <u>and</u> take away." "I guess God is good <u>and</u> sometimes bad." This is the only explanation that a works-focused religious person can come up with: It is someone else's fault. Satan misuses the book of Job to direct all of that blame toward God.

Why does the desire for ease and rest dominate our thinking?

For most people, the desire to have comfort amidst the difficulties in their lives overrides God's call to pursue Him through the difficulties. There is one real test on this earth: Will we trust God?" How many of us should be somewhere other than where we are right now? We should have different relationships or be in a different environment in order to be equipped to fulfill God's plan for our lives. Most of the time the reason we do not follow through with God's leading is that we simply do not trust Him. Our desire for ease, like Job, has clouded our understanding of God's love. God wants us to know that we can trust Him.

As Christians we will suffer persecutions in this life. If we continue in our pursuit of God this will cause friction because we will be going opposite to this world's system. Also, bad things can occur as the consequence of sin's entrance into our world. We must decide whether we are going to be deceived into blaming God for bad circumstances or believe the truth that He is good and continue to pursue Him.

I believe the number one reason we stop pursuing God is the day to day struggle of life. *"Now he who received seed among the thorns is he who hears the word, and <u>the cares of this world</u> and <u>the deceitfulness of riches</u> choke the word, and he becomes unfruitful"* (Matthew 13:22). The simple mundane situations of life that we must go through can stifle what really matters: our relationship with God. Remember, we were created for a place where things work out. God never planned for us to struggle through all these obstacles. In our fallen world we must consciously decide to push through these obstacles to know God.

People who know the God of love are no longer dismayed by life's struggles.

If we refuse false comfort and push through to know God, we are given the understanding of His goodness. This knowledge of God's goodness enables us to transcend the problems of this life. People who know the God of love are no longer dismayed by life's struggles. There is power in the knowledge of God's love for us. God's love is the only foundation for our Christian faith. Sometimes we can even become fixated on our own ability to have faith in God. It is so easy for us to get diverted from trusting only in God's love that we can start to have faith in our own ability to have faith. Our enemy, the devil, will do whatever it takes to get our reliance on anything other than trusting in God's love for us.

How do we avoid being deceived?

Any personal confusion will work itself out if we start with the foundation of God's love.

God cannot act outside of His character which is love (1 John 4:16). *"Love suffers long and is kind; love does not envy; love does not parade itself, is not puffed up; does not behave rudely, does not seek its own, is not provoked, thinks no evil; does not rejoice in iniquity, but rejoices in the truth; bears all things, believes all things, hopes all things, endures all things. Love never fails"* (1 Corinthians 13:4-8a). If we are uncertain of what to believe, we must rely on the unchanging foundation of

God's goodness. Any personal confusion will work itself out if we start with the foundation of God's love.

God loves Job and God loves us. The simple difference between our relationship with God and Job's relationship is that Job did not have the available resources to understand God that we now have. Job's fear ran the course of his life for a while, but after meeting God he came into an abundant life free from fear. This was the end that God intended which is spoken of in James 5:11. The knowledge of God's love casts out fear (1 John 4:18). God never caused the tragedies that came on Job!

Jesus had no tolerance for people who followed Him for what they could get from Him. He said some abrasive things to those people, *"Then Jesus said to them, "Most assuredly, 'I say to you, <u>unless you eat the flesh of the Son of Man and drink His blood</u>, you have no life in you'"* (John 6:53). God requires us to follow Him by faith, even when it does not make sense. **God is good whether we have proof in our current situation or not.** God's desire is that we learn to live by faith and not our own understanding (Proverbs 3:5).

God wants our relationship with Him to develop to the point that our trust of Him transcends our confusion.

God knew when the book of Job was written that His enemy would use it to confuse many people, yet He did not stop it from being written. In God's omniscience, He foresaw all the misguidance that would come from people who would explain the book of Job from their own misunderstandings of His character. God was not deterred because He is looking for people who will pursue Him personally and not follow Him based on someone else's opinion. God is not interested in second hand relationships.

Summarizing the Powerful Lessons from Job

God wants our relationship with Him to develop to the point that our trust of Him transcends our confusion. <u>The trouble is that most people quit when the relationship is no longer easy.</u> Also many people are happy to receive second hand revelation about God because it is easier than personal pursuit. Most of the misconceptions about God's actions in the book of Job come from people accepting second hand revelation. Jesus spoke many parables which were probably only understood by the people who continued to replay them in their mind until they received His deeper meaning. Be the person who will not quit until you have received personal confirmation from the Holy Spirit about a particular truth. God loves your pursuit of Him because He loves you!

God does not give answers to people who believe they deserve them. God gives answers to people who will not quit until they know Him.

When you study the Bible take a moment to ponder how omniscient God is. He knows what scripture we will be reading and He knows that we may not understand it immediately. We are not to be overwhelmed by our inability to understand, just continue to pursue the answer. God loves that we want to know Him. God does not give answers to people who believe they deserve them. God gives answers to people who will not quit until they know Him.

Don't be confused about the Question: "Why did God allow it?"

The significance of the rebellion of man in the Garden of Eden is underestimated because most people do not understand delegated authority. The higher the position of authority, the more damage is caused when someone misuses the authority which was entrusted to them. God gave man dominion or authority over all the earth (Genesis 1:28). Knowing the integrity of God leads us to recognize that He will <u>never</u> violate His word and He gave us our authority by His word. Most of the time God is not <u>causing</u> something; He is simply not intervening because we have been given the authority in that area. The real problem is: <u>we do not believe we have the authority that He gave us</u>.

We can become angry at injustice because no wrong was ever meant to happen. Every tragedy should have never taken place! The real frustration is this: why does so much bad happen if it is not supposed to happen? Bad things happen every day that are outside of the will of God. This is not because God is powerless, it is due to His having entrusted us with authority on the earth.

The assumption that God can randomly intervene whenever He so chooses is actually in opposition to God's word. This assumption cunningly implies that God is able to go against His Own word, while the truth is that this will never happen. The rebellion of Adam and Eve, who partook of the tree of the knowledge of good and evil, brought with it the enticing desire to use our free will to choose evil and not good. This also set the pattern for blaming God. In Adam's first meeting with God after he had sinned, he shifted the blame to God for the women He had given him (Genesis 3:12). Satan is more than willing to use these evil enticements, along with his lies, to draw people toward wrong decisions. Mankind's continued obedience to God's command in the Garden of Eden would have avoided all of this. Now, the daily ramifications of the evil choices of many are simply a fact of our fallen world.

Summarizing the Powerful Lessons from Job

God has given each of us authority and this authority causes us to have influence over others. Delegation of authority always brings with it the ability to influence others for good or for evil. Adam and Eve were given authority over all of the earth along with the authority to reproduce and thereby multiply the human race (Genesis 1:28). It is very clear that Adam and Eve were God's appointed and delegated authority over all of the earth. Therefore, their rebellion, through sin, negatively influenced everything under their authority. Adam and Eve's rebellion forever altered the human experience. Their descendants now have the ability to reproduce evil. They also have a clouded view of their own authority along with a misunderstanding of God Who gave them their authority.

To truly change the world for good means using our influence to inspire and encourage others to come into a personal relationship with God which will result in their submission to His Lordship. Once in this relationship, we are able to be led by God so He can once again accomplish His loving will on the earth as it was in the beginning. As God's trusting ambassadors, we who believe in His words are able to overcome evil on this earth.

The authority we have been given in Christ is much more powerful than most of us realize. Our authority is activated by faith in God and is apparently unlimited. *"So Jesus answered and said to them, 'Have faith in God. For assuredly, I say to you, whoever says to this mountain, 'Be removed and be cast into the sea,' and does not doubt in his heart, but believes that those things he says will be done, he will have whatever he says. Therefore I say to you, whatever things you ask when you pray, believe that you receive them, and you will have them'"* (Mark 11:22-24)

As we advance in technical achievements, the contrast of the increase of human depravity only serves to remind us that mental achievements never ensure the needed spiritual/moral change which our world is lacking. Only love can make this world what it was intended to be, and true love can only flourish under the authority of God. Anyone who is not submitted to the God of love will succumb to the influences of evil which operate outside the authority of God.

What is the most practical way to see the truth about Job?

The most practical way to understand Job is the simple concept of comparing Job's words with David's words. This one idea has helped many people to see that there is something wrong with Job's understanding. This comparison serves to remove Job from the pious spiritual pedestal upon which he should never have been placed. After Job is dethroned, it becomes much easier to see the truths that God is trying to reveal through the book of Job.

Other than Jesus's relationship with the Father, David is simply the best model of relationship with God that is available to us in the Bible. Because David's words are grounded in relationship and not law, they are the perfect comparison to Job's words in order to obtain an accurate understanding. David does not tie his relationship with God to his performance. This becomes a vital key to understanding the book of Job. It also becomes the key to understanding the unconditional acceptance that we have in Christ. God loves us regardless of our performance. David knew this and Job did not.

Summarizing the Powerful Lessons from Job

Why should we live by faith and not by answers?

What truth you choose to receive from the lessons in Job's story is up to you. If you choose not to embrace God's goodness, then Job's story will not have God's intended effect upon you. Job 42:11 is one of the saddest verses in this book, *"Then all his brothers, all his sisters, and all those who had been his acquaintances before, came to him and ate food with him in his house; and they consoled him and comforted him <u>for all the adversity that the LORD had brought upon him</u>. Each one gave him a piece of silver and each a ring of gold."* **The only person in this story that appears to have changed is Job — the one who met God.** All of Job's acquaintances still believed that God brought the adversity (<u>evil</u> in the KJV version) upon him. Job's faith had been changed by his personal encounter with the God of love. Without a personal encounter, the others' understanding has remained unaffected. This emphasizes the critical point that everyone's relationship with God is individualistic and can never be built on another's relationship. <u>Pursue God for yourself and never settle for only the revelation of someone else's relationship</u>.

To meet God is to experience His goodness.

Although I have stated it several times, it is important that we review this critical point. Our faith must rest on the foundation of the goodness of God or it does not even qualify for faith. *"But without faith it is impossible to please Him, for he who comes to God must believe that He is, and that <u>He is a rewarder</u> of those who diligently seek Him"* (Hebrews 11:6). After Job's encounter, he is no longer acknowledging a God whom he does not know, but One he has personally met. To meet God is to experience His goodness. Please humble yourself as a little child to receive the simplicity of the foundation of faith: God is good. *"Assuredly,*

I say to you, whoever does not receive the kingdom of God as a little child will by no means enter it" (Mark 10:15).

God cannot be both good and evil or He would be working against Himself. Jesus said, *"If a kingdom is divided against itself, that kingdom cannot stand"* (Mark 3:24). Good cannot produce evil. Jesus said, *"Even so, every good tree bears good fruit, but a bad tree bears bad fruit. A good tree cannot bear bad fruit, nor can a bad tree bear good fruit"* (Matthew 7:17-18). We also find the same principle in the book of James, *"Does a spring send forth fresh water and bitter from the same opening? Can a fig tree, my brethren, bear olives, or a grapevine bear figs? Thus no spring yields both salt water and fresh"* (James 3:11-12).

When we get to heaven we will not have the revelation that God was meaner than we thought!

The foundation of all truth is that the Lord is good: Psalm 34:8, 100:5, 106:1, 107:1, 118:1, 118:29, 135:3, 136:1, and 145:9. Every evil power is attempting to destroy our understanding of God's goodness. *"For the weapons of our warfare are not carnal but mighty in God for pulling down strongholds, casting down arguments and every high thing __that exalts itself against the knowledge of God__, bringing every thought into captivity to the obedience of Christ"* (2 Corinthians 10:4-6). We must choose to resist any deception, no matter the source, that attempts to undermine the goodness of our God.

When we get to heaven we will not have the revelation that God was meaner than we thought! We will be shocked at how little we comprehended the depth of His love for us. *"For I am persuaded that neither death nor life, nor angels nor principalities nor powers, nor things present nor things to come, nor height nor depth, nor any other created thing, shall be able to separate us from the love of God which is in Christ Jesus our Lord"* (Romans 8:38-39).

The end of the story.

"Now the LORD blessed the latter days of Job more than his beginning; for he had fourteen thousand sheep, six thousand camels, one thousand yoke of oxen, and one thousand female donkeys. He also had seven sons and three daughters. And he called the name of the first Jemimah, the name of the second Keziah, and the name of the third Keren-Happuch. In all the land were found no women so beautiful as the daughters of Job; and their father gave them an inheritance among their brothers. After this Job lived one hundred and forty years, and saw his children and grandchildren for four generations. So Job died, old and full of days." (Job 42:12-16)

PRAYER

Father, we thank you for the book of Job as part of Your full counsel to us. We thank You for the understanding You have given that reveals how closely we are like our brother, Job. Father, we know that You have not hidden things from us so that we will not find them, but so that we will find them. We thank you for your promise in Jeremiah 29:13-14a, *"And you will seek Me and find Me, when you search for Me with all your heart. I will be found by you, says the LORD."* Father, please help us to continue our search no matter the circumstances, that we might know the love of Christ which passes knowledge, that we may be filled with all the fullness of God. Amen.

EXTENDED OUTLINE

Chapter 1 Why is This Love Letter Under Attack?   17
Why is God's character the key?   17
Why is the book of Job relevant today?   18
What makes Job the most unique book of the Bible?   19
How much of the book of Job can be used to establish doctrine?   21
Why are we prone to doubt God's goodness?   24
What is Satan's strategy?   25
How is man honored by God?   27

Chapter 2 Why is the Meaning of "Sovereignty" a Target?   29
Who is responsible for distorting the concept of sovereignty?   29
How is sovereignty used to divide us?   30
Why did God allow it?   32
Why didn't God intervene?   34
What about the filter of God's will?   35
Why do bad things happen to good people?   36
Why do we underestimate the effects of our rebellion?   38

Chapter 3 Why Do We Long to Trust God?   43
Where did Job's desire for rest come from?   43
What is wrong with wanting life to be easy?   46
How can tragedy affect us?   48
Reading Job's story   49
What kind of relationship does Job have with God?   54
Why compare Job's relationship with God to David's?   56

Chapter 4 Is it God's Fault?   59
Why do we blame God?   59
What are the limitations of a sovereign God?   60
What is delegated authority?   62
Why does God delegate authority?   63
How does false sovereignty clash with the real world?   64
Does someone have to be guilty?   66
What undermines our relationship with God the most?   67
How fast can our desire for rest be tested?   69
How does Satan use the book of Job most effectively?   71

Chapter 5 How Does God Deal With Our Deceived Hearts?   75
How does God guide us when our understanding is the biggest obstacle? 75

What do we do when bad things happen?	77
Why are we double-minded?	80
Has God run out of options with Job?	81
Why must God take us through our fears?	82
Do our fears have the power to change our future?	83
What does God's commendation of Job reveal about their relationship?	85

Chapter 6   What is Job's Mindset?   91

Why is Job not listed in the hall of faith in Hebrews 11?	91
What is commitment doctrine and how do we recognize it?	92
What are some examples of commitment doctrine?	94
How can our own integrity be used against us?	96
What is Job's limited view of his relationship with God?	98
Can God be both good and bad?	100
How does an unpredictable God affect Job's desire for rest?	103
Is Job avoiding relationship by embracing sovereignty?	105

Chapter 7   How Can We Understand Theology Through Relationship?   109

How old is the concept of relationship?	109
What happened relationally when man rebelled against God?	110
Why is Paul a good example of resting in relationship?	111
How do we learn to rest and not fear?	112
Why is David a good example of resting in relationship?	113
How does relationship triumph over the law?	115
How does relationship triumph over dispensation?	117
What is God's easy yoke and light burden?	118
How easy is it to trust in ourselves?	120
How do we keep a proper perspective?	121

Chapter 8   What is True Rest?   123

How is Hebrews a book about rest?	123
Why should our motive for pursing God be relationship?	123
What rest is Hebrews talking about?	126
What is the root cause of disobedience?	127
Why did God institute a Sabbath rest?	128
Can someone have faith without rest?	129
What does thankfulness have to do with rest?	131
What does God consider to be most important?	132
Does Job have a pride issue?	134
Why is relinquishing leadership of our lives an ongoing decision?	136

Chapter 9   Vital Life Lessons from Job   139

What are God's warnings about material blessings?	139
How can purposely remembering help our perspective?	143

What does Job's thought process teach us?	145
How far can our desire for rest lead us?	146
Why doesn't God just show up and tell Job He loves him?	147
How are we to understand God's jealousy?	148
What is the correct way to receive revelation from God's word?	149
What can the book of Job teach us about friendship?	150
What happens when answers become our god?	152

Chapter 10   Job's Confessions of Confusion — 155

Why should we count the blessings of our time?	155
How should we fight against works-focused religion?	155
When did Job's heart change toward God?	157
What is the deepest desire of Job's heart?	159
Does Jobs commitment have him trapped?	159
Does Job's venting at God bring him relief?	161
Why do Job's accusations turn to demands?	162
Why are we aware of an island of truth in Job's sea of confusion?	162
Why does Job vacillate on the wicked being punished?	164
What is the foundation for Job's defense?	166
Why did Job lose his incentive for serving God?	167

Chapter 11   Explaining Controversial Passages in Job — Part 1 — 169

How do we address the apparent contradictions in Job?	169
What about God's declaration that Job is right?	170
What about the hedge around Job?	171
Is Job trusting in his performance?	173
Was Job right about adversity coming from God?	175
Did God send fire down from heaven?	176
Did the wind that killed Job's children come from God?	178
How will works-focused religion fail?	181

Chapter 12   Job Meets God — 183

Why has Job's quest for answers not worked?	183
Is Elihu a mediator?	184
Do Elihu and God agree on Job's problem?	186
Why does Elihu proclaim God's majesty?	187
Is God angry with Job?	189
Was Job's foundation himself?	190
Why does Job change so quickly?	192

Chapter 13   Explaining Controversial Passages in Job — Part 2 — 195

What about Elihu's difficult statement?	195
What about God's incitement against Job?	196
Does God allow Satan access to Job?	197

Does Satan's accusation of Job prove to be true?	198
Is God validating the statements of Job?	200

Chapter 14 Summarizing the Powerful Lessons from Job — **203**

Why do most people think like Job?	203
Why does the desire for ease and rest dominate our thinking?	204
How do we avoid being deceived?	205
Don't be confused about the question: "Why did God allow it?"	207
What is the most practical way to see the truth about Job?	210
Why should we live by faith and not by answers?	211
The end of the story	213

Prayer — **215**

ABOUT THE AUTHOR

I grew up in the Christian church and accepted Jesus as my savior at the age of seven, but did not find myself growing very much spiritually as I got older. Even after re-dedicating my life to God at the age of twenty-one I still did not feel close to God. I was attending church and doing all of the right things. In fact, I was one of the best doers there, but something was missing. There just had to be more to the Christian life.

I started my own service business in 1990 and by 2000 I could do my work and, at the same time, think on something completely different. So, while working I would meditate on bible verses. It was during one of these extended times of thinking on a particular passage of scripture that something began to happen.

For years I would think on 1 Corinthians 2:16 "For who has known the mind of the Lord that he may instruct Him? But we have the mind of Christ." I did not see any immediate changes, but I can look back now and see that one specific thought began to permeate my mind: God loved me. I found myself, even on very difficult days of demanding physical labor, being assured that no matter what I was going through; God loved me. I now know I was experiencing the foundational understanding of the mind of Christ. I was receiving the knowledge of God's love.

As this revelation was growing I began to see that other Christians, for the most part, did not have this assurance of God's love. I found myself saying all the time, "It's ok, God loves you." But, I knew I had to do more. Sometime around the summer of 2009 God directed me to attend Charis Bible College in Colorado Springs, Colorado. In the spring of 2013 I founded The Truth Wins Ministries, which is dedicated to overcoming the opposing forces that suppress the knowledge of God's love. This book is the second in a series devoted to that purpose.